BOOKS BY WILLIAM McILWAIN

Legends of Baptist Hollow
(IN COLLABORATION)

The Glass Rooster

Naked Came the Stranger
(IN COLLABORATION)

A FAREWELL TO ALCOHOL

A FAREWELL
TO ALCOHOL

William McIlwain

Random House, New York

Library of Congress Cataloging in Publication Data
McIlwain, William.
  A farewell to alcohol.
  1. Alcoholics—Personal narratives. 2. Alcoholism—Treatment.
  I. Title.
HV5293.M17A5   362.2′92′0924   [B]   72–5121
ISBN 0-394-47610-7

Manufactured in the United States of America
by Haddon Craftsman, Scranton, Penna.

9 8 7 6 5 4 3 2
First Edition

For Harold Hayes

Much of this book was written in letters
to a close friend.
That's why it is divided into days,
rather than chapters.

Butner, North Carolina

Tuesday

✄

I WAS LATE GETTING TO BUTNER TODAY AND THEY
wouldn't let me in. The psychiatrist in Winston-Salem
had told me to get here at ten-thirty A.M., but he
hadn't made a special point of it, and I couldn't see
where time made much difference. I got out of bed
around nine o'clock, fixed a vodka and orange juice,
and drank it while reading the sports pages. I had told
the children the night before that I was going to the
Alcoholic Rehabilitation Center. All three of them
were pleased. After I finished the sports pages, I fixed
another vodka and orange juice and drank it while
talking with my wife. We have agreed to end our marriage and we talked a long while.

Around eleven I decided it was time to go, and I
fixed a cup of black coffee and a vodka and orange
juice to drink while I shaved and showered. I had never

3

been to the ARC, or any other institution, and I wasn't sure what I would need. Deciding it would be casual, I packed two bags of sports clothes, my bathing suit, an alarm clock, a briefcase full of supplies, my typewriter, an unfinished magazine article that I am writing, two tennis rackets, a hundred newspapers that I have agreed to study for a publisher for $1,500, and nine books—*Slaughterhouse-Five*, *The Crackup* by Scott Fitzgerald, *Immortal Poems of the English Language*, *Diary of a Mad Housewife*, *People in Quandaries* by Wendell Johnson, *Editor and Publisher Yearbook* (I am a newspaperman), *The New American Webster Handy College Dictionary*, *The Penal Colony* by Kafka, and *Romantic Poets* in the Viking Portable edition. I thought that would be all I needed. I wasn't sure whether drunks played tennis, but I would have an extra racket if I found one who did.

I got to Butner around one-thirty and stopped at a pool hall, drinking a tall Schlitz while watching three games of eight-ball. None of the men could shoot well. I didn't have a particular feeling that this beer would be the last one I'd ever drink, but I mused over it. I got to the Alcoholic Rehabilitation Center around two-fifteen and told the lady who I was. "Bill," she said, "you're late." "I know it," I said, "I'm sorry. I left late." "Bill, you're four hours late." She was beginning to annoy me calling me "Bill"—she didn't know me and I wasn't a small-time drunk. "I'm sorry," I said. "Bill, you'll have to come back next week," she said. "I can't take you." I almost said, "The hell with it, lady," but something strong made me know that I had to get into Butner. If I went away, I wouldn't ever come back. "Can I get a motel and get in tomorrow?" "Bill, you'll just drink all night and then we can't let you in." "No, ma'am, I won't do that. I really need to get in here." "Do you have any friends in AA you could spend the night with?" "No, ma'am." Finally she said well, maybe a person scheduled to report the next day might cancel out. I could call her in the morning and see.

I went to the liquor store in Creedmoor, bought a fifth of vodka, and got a motel room beside a muddy pond. I had a few vodka and Sprites and fixed another to carry to an outside phone booth. I hated to do it, but I was going to call the woman. I told her how much I appreciated her consideration and I hoped someone would cancel tomorrow. I was taking a nap when the motel manager came down and knocked (there are no phones in the rooms) and said, "The lady at ARC said she'll take you in the morning."

I dressed, put my vodka in the car and decided to ride around Butner. It would be the last chance I would have to see all of it. Butner was an army camp, near Durham, North Carolina, during World War II and now it is a vast State of North Carolina complex that includes the John Umsted Hospital, a huge green-topped structure for mental patients and bad drunks; a center for retarded children; a school for the blind; a center for youthful offenders; a farm; and the Alcoholic Rehabilitation Center. The center is one of three in North Carolina, operated by the State Department of Mental Health.

Across from the hospital, a softball game was going on, and I saw a black centerfielder turn on a fly ball and take it on the run, almost at the fence. A little later, the leftfielder, white, did almost the same thing. I thought that these must be the crazy people because drunks can't catch fly balls. I could still hit when I quit playing softball, but I couldn't judge a fly ball. I was getting a little drunk now and I saw some deep significance in this—the crazy people being able to catch fly balls. I watched until the game ended at almost dark and drove back to the motel. I sat in a chair and drank all of the vodka except three drinks. I wanted to have those in the morning before I went to the Alcoholic Center.

Wednesday

><

I WOKE UP SWEATING AND SHIVERING AND FEELING AS if I were choking. In the old days, drinking a fifth of vodka at night wouldn't do this to me, but it does now because I have been drinking a long time. Some of the ice hadn't melted, and I thought if I could drink a vodka and Sprite, I might quit sweating and shivering. I drank two and still felt bad when I stopped at a restaurant. It wasn't officially open but the man and his wife were pleasant. He said I could have a bowl of Brunswick stew for breakfast, if I liked that. I ate the Brunswick stew, drinking the last vodka and Sprite that I had. I did wonder now if this would be the last drink I would ever have. "You going to be around a few days?" the restaurant man asked. "I'm going to the ARC," I said. He hesitated and said, "Good luck." I thanked him, finished the drink, and left the motel glass on his table.

"Well, Bill," the lady at ARC said, "you look a lot better this morning. I'm glad." I thanked her and said, "Yes, ma'am, I feel a lot better today." She filled out some forms, asked my income, studied a while, and said, "Bill, I'm going to have to charge you thirty-two dollars a day." It was more than I had expected and later I learned that many of my fellow patients were paying four dollars a day, some of them one dollar a day, but that's fair enough. Certainly in a program such as this, a patient should pay only what he can afford.

A bearded young doctor, a good sport, examined me, studying my retinas, pushing at my liver, and seeing whether I could distinguish between sharp and dull objects when they touched my legs. "Were you a wrestler?" he asked. I thought he meant a well-built college wrestler and I felt good; then I thought he meant a professional wrestler with a big belly. My waistline gradually got bigger as I escalated to keeping a half-gallon of vodka at home, a half-gallon in my office, and a half-gallon in the trunk of my car, in case I got caught away from home or the office. I was drinking about seven Sprites a day with the vodka and also eating, which many alcoholics don't do. I told him no, but I had been a football player. It was a long examination, and I felt ashamed of being so shaky and wet with perspiration. I left feeling better, though, because he said, "You have great lungs."

It was hot outside and a long way from my car to C Dorm, one of the three single-story brick buildings where patients live, about twenty to a dorm. Sweating,

I struggled with the two bags of clothing, the type-writer, the two tennis rackets, the briefcase, and the hundred newspapers. I had to make three trips. In the lobby of C Dorm, I saw men and women, black and white, sitting together in chairs and on a couch watching television and playing cards. A beautiful black woman and a young white man—attendants—put my bags on a bed and went through them, taking Listerine, Bufferin, nose drops, and iodine. They would have taken shaving lotion and hair tonic, but I didn't have any.

"We'll give these back when you leave," the woman said.

"You have to leave your car at the police station," the young man said. "I'll follow you over after lunch and drive you back."

"You should go now," the woman said, "and eat with the rest of them."

I am at Butner, then—"with the rest of them"—and we include all sorts: Tommy Morgan (I will not use patients' real names), who dropped out of college eight months ago because "I was drinking so much I couldn't keep up with my studies"; a small trucker who cannot read or write; a grandmother who drinks vanilla extract; a young man who writes detective stories and has written a good book; Tip Watson, who constructed a whiskey still when he was fourteen, sold its output at a nearby sawmill, and began drinking it, too; a business executive's wife, Julie Ryan, who has twice tried to commit suicide; a mathematician, highly articulate; Mr. Wellington, a boy scout leader and "secret drinker"; Ellen Hill, who drank only beer; a truck driver who was using amphetamines and whiskey at the same time; and Mr. Leland, who for years would get in his boat and go across the river to buy a half-gallon of moonshine. Mr. Leland's words are difficult to understand; he mumbles, batting his eyes steadily, shaking so much that he can hardly lift a cup of coffee to his mouth.

There is, perhaps, only one similarity in us all: none of us thought he would ever become an alcoholic, but all of us have become alcoholics.

Tommy Morgan, a large, good-looking boy with a beard, held open the dorm door to let me out, then held the cafeteria door to let me in. He has only a week more to stay here and he looks fine. "After I dropped out of school," he said, "I started working on logging jobs. Some mornings I would wake up in the woods. I would be drunk and cold and scared to death. I wouldn't know where I was." Tommy is C Dorm leader, elected by the patients, and he runs the morning meetings in the dorm, makes clean-up assignments, and helps patients in any way that he can. He ate lunch with me and two other new patients who came today to the dorm—Tip Watson and Paul Evans. Paul said he was reared in a "churchgoing family" but began drinking beer, three tall six-packs a day toward the end, and finally lost his wife and grocery store. It is his first time at ARC. Tip has been here several times, and this morning he came over from the "Big Top"

(John Umstead Hospital), where he had spent a week getting over the d.t.'s.

"Lord, Lord," he said, "I was over there with those crazy people. I hadn't smoked for a year and it got me smoking again."

After lunch I sat on a green bench in front of the dorm and talked with other patients. It is a strange feeling to be here. I drank whiskey many years—successfully, you could say—and I never thought I would have to come to a center for alcoholics.

Looking back on it, I believe I understand some of what happened to me. I took my first drink of anything (beer) when I was an eighteen-year-old Marine Corps private, standing beside Frank Dassori, a good person, at Camp LeJeune, North Carolina. I had started my career as a newspaperman a year earlier, working nights as a high school senior, and I rose steadily in the profession. I did my work well, but it was not always accompanied by a feeling of ease. In time, I turned to whiskey for that ease, and gradually, over the years, I drank more. I continued to work well. For a long while.

From Camp LeJeune to Butner, twenty-seven years, my career as a drinker-newspaperman was this: Attending college after World War II, I went for long periods without even thinking about whiskey. But on occasion, I drank a great deal, the occasion being a dance or a party or, once, a mock trial in which a student was sentenced to be hanged. (A law student loosened the bathrobe cord before the boy strangled.) I wrote steadily for newspapers, covering sports events during the college year and working full time during the summer. I was not concerned about how real my talents were—I felt they were considerable—and certainly I was not concerned about whiskey ever becoming a problem.

That pattern held true for several years after college, but in Richmond, Virginia, working on the *Times-Dispatch*, I began to feel the uneasiness that would grow. I had just married and was living what would be considered the good life of a successful young reporter. But I recall a night driving fast through the countryside, close on deadline, going to cover a triple-murder fifty miles away, and thinking, for an instant: If I hit that bridge abutment, I won't have to cover it. That didn't make sense. I was being acclaimed in that city and I could read my stories and tell that they were good. It had begun, an almost mystical process in which I would always succeed, but at great cost— *seeing* the success but wondering how I had brought it about, wondering if I could do it again. But I never went to my apartment and thought: I've got to have a drink. A fifth of bourbon would last for weeks.

I accepted a job at *Newsday* in 1954 and my wife and I moved to Long Island, where the first of our three children was born two months later. My work and drinking patterns at *Newsday* were much as they had been in Richmond. At least for many years. I succeeded: chief copy editor, day news editor, city editor, assistant managing editor, managing editor, editor. I felt many days and nights, though, as if I were doing it with mirrors: not using the real skills of a professional but skills less concrete, less admirable, perhaps little more than the native cunning and charm of a Southerner who could praise, humor, pamper, and reason men and women above and beneath him into doing, finally, what he wanted done. I rarely ordered anyone to do anything. And I rarely made it known when anyone—again, *above* or *beneath* me— hurt me or caused me difficulty with a thoughtless act. I told myself that I acted this way because it was effective and because I was a good-natured person.

Still, for at least ten years, I did not drink much each day. I might have two drinks at lunch or dinner, but even that was not a steady practice. At times, though, as in college, I would drink for hours, great amounts. It might be a dinner meeting with other editors to work out a tough problem or make some great change at *Newsday*. Or it might be an editors' convention in San Francisco or Washington, where I had bloody Marys at breakfast, cocktails throughout the day, and whiskey, gin, or vodka far into the night. Always I behaved well, was articulate (more articulate, actually), and recalled the next day precisely what had been said and done, by myself and everyone around me. Maybe if I had got sick or done something really stupid in those years, I would have become alarmed.

I didn't. I went on drinking, gradually more because it was accepted on my newspaper, remaining the man who could hold whiskey, a good-natured editor who didn't rebuke anyone. But wishing, too, that I *had* rebuked someone, this thought coming as I drove twenty miles at night to my home, wishing I had said to a news editor: Look, you're getting paid to do your job the same way I'm getting paid to do mine. Don't sit here like a damn kid resisting everything in sight. I told you to quit jumping so many stories and I goddamn well expect you to do it. But I never said that. The next day there would be five jumps (continued stories) when I had wanted no more than two.

I had a refrigerator put in my office, would play tennis at lunchtime, come back and eat a can of cold tuna fish and drink vodka and tonic. I would lay off the vodka a few hours and start again shortly before the seven P.M. news conference in my office. Later I quit laying off the few hours; I would begin drinking after tennis, drink through the news conference, and then sit alone in my office and drink a while, thinking, before I began my ride home. I realized the degree to which my home life had deteriorated: little was left except love for my two daughters and my son, and that was being eroded, too, by absence and conversation that too often was empty.

I did not realize, though, what was happening to me professionally. Bill Moyers, who had become publisher of *Newsday* in 1968, spoke to me about drinking so much—gently at first, sometimes in a kidding way, but later in a more concerned fashion. I paid little attention to him, thinking that he simply had been associated with more conventional people during his years as press secretary and special assistant to President Johnson. I felt Bill would have to accept my drinking and my brilliance; I had helped make *News-*

day one of the finest newspapers in the world and I had done it while drinking. I believe now—but didn't then—that I was becoming paralyzed in my job, a drunk figurehead who no longer was making great contributions to my newspaper. Gradually, though, that fear was creeping into my mind. I would entertain it long enough to feel concern, remorse, depression—then reject it with great resentment. The hell with Bill Moyers and anybody else who doesn't think I'm still one of the two or three best editors in the United States. But I was frightened, also growing tired of the struggle.

Moyers, without my knowledge, arranged what amounted to an ultra-white-collar firing: my becoming writer-in-residence for a year at Wake Forest University on full salary. Out of pride and anger, I had to take the job—but I saw it, too, as a chance; maybe there I could make a new start. But my year at the university (1970–71) turned out no better than my later days at *Newsday*. I drank steadily, beginning most days when I awoke around noon, made bad starts on two novels and succeeded in writing an article for *Harper's* and another for *Esquire* only because it was write them or admit total collapse. That—and the great concern of *Esquire's* editor, Harold Hayes, who worked more carefully with me than any editor should ever have to with a professional writer. I was at the end of the string. I would wake up in the morning shivering and sweating, frightened, knowing where my life was headed. I would drink before breakfast to ease those feelings, never totally, drink all day, and begin the next day the same way.

Except when asleep, I could not go an hour without drinking. My clothes had been outgrown because of fat; I had hit myself twice in the head with a steel racket, playing tennis while drunk; I was accomplishing nothing as a writer; what companionship I was still trying, feebly, to offer my children, whom I love, was worthless. At forty-five I did not like what I was. I did not, in fact, like what I had ever been. I was drawn deeply to a beautiful young girl, less than half my age —clutching desperately at first, I believe, for hope of change. Any change. But as the relationship grew, I saw what I must try to become.

On an early spring afternoon at Hanes Park, in Winston-Salem, North Carolina, I saw a man about my age playing tennis with his two sons. He was slender, tanned, and seemed happy. My sister-in-law said he was a business executive, well known in town, who had just returned from Butner. My wife urged me to consider going. I talked with Dr. Richard C. Proctor, chairman of psychiatry at Bowman Gray School of Medicine. He is one of the region's top men on alcoholism. Dr. Proctor said he knew of patients who had gone to Butner and found good lives; he knew of others who had stopped and got drunk on the way home. He made the telephone calls that arranged for me to be admitted.

I am here, then, a man who has failed as a husband and as a father and as a newspaperman. Those scars are deep. I am intelligent enough to know that whatever brought those failures, whatever led me to alcoholism, is still a part of me. But I know, too, that I have great will—curiously, I have *always* had great will, even when I didn't exercise it—and I believe that I shall succeed.

Thursday

⋈

I GOT UP AT FIVE-THIRTY A.M. TO TAKE A BLOOD TEST, then spent most of the morning sitting on one of the benches in front of the dorm. On sunny days, during "free time," patients sit out front and talk steadily of whiskey. Other things might be discussed, but almost always the conversation leads to whiskey.

In early afternoon I was walking around the quadrangle, a quarter-mile of white sidewalk encompassing grass and pine trees, when I was intercepted by a young woman in a miniskirt. "I'm Dr. Corder," she said. "I know you just got here, but do you feel like taking some tests?"

I didn't feel like it, but I told her that I would. We went to her office in one of the low brick buildings and she got out the material. The first test was IQ and I felt jumpy. This was particularly true on the sections involving numbers, which I have never been good at, and blocks. The idea of the blocks, red and white, was to arrange them quickly in designs exactly like those on cards that Dr. Corder showed me. I missed a good many of those, not being able to finish them in time. On vocabulary and logic, it was as if someone else were answering the questions and getting them right. Even as I answered, I was thinking of something that a girl had told me before I came here: that I undoubtedly had suffered brain damage from drinking as much as I have. As I heard myself answering the vocabulary words correctly, I wondered what that meant. Maybe I hadn't been able to work the blocks because of brain damage; and now maybe it was just an old reflex doing the job for me on vocabulary. I wondered about that.

"You did extremely well," Dr. Corder said. "Will you take some reaction tests for me?"

I didn't feel good about that, either. I once had quick reflexes and good timing, but I knew some of that had left me. I had been in a bar on Long Island with a friend one night and we got to fooling with a game machine that had two buttons. The point was to press a button with one hand, which would release a falling object, then press the other button in time to halt the object before it reached the bottom of its course. He was stopping it about halfway; I tried three times, not stopping it at all twice and, the other time, stopping it just barely before the bottom.

Dr. Corder and I went to a testing room in the administration building and she explained how the test would work. Two fingers of my left hand and two fingers of my right hand would rest on a keyboard with the numbers 2, 3, 4, 5. A board in front of me had corresponding numbers. A red light would flash, indicating that soon number 2, 3, 4, or 5 would light up in white. As it came on, I must press the right number on my keyboard. If I got it right, a green light would flash. It seemed to me that it was going to be a lot like that game machine. It turned out, though, to be a simple matter, with plenty of time between lights. But the test lasted an hour, and sometimes my concentration would falter and I would punch a 3 rather than a 2, or a 4 rather than a 5. I thought I did pretty well.

I asked Dr. Corder if she thought I would ever fly a jet fighter or play the piano. She said the computer would have to study my work.

This is a quiet place. About seventy-five patients is capacity, meaning there aren't many moving figures. A dozen to twenty other patients are kept in D Dorm, the "lock ward" at John Umstead Hospital, a mile away, but they don't eat or sleep here. They are brought by bus for lectures and films. Patients can walk only as far as the street in front of the administration building or the edge of nearby woods on the other three sides. (After spending seven nights at ARC, a patient—accompanied by an attendant—can go to the barber shop or beauty parlor, or go shopping. Normally, one person collects money, makes a list, and shops for an entire dorm.) The grounds aren't large and they look the same, hour after hour, because nothing is happening. A new patient, carrying a bag or paper sacks, draws attention as he moves down the white walks. So does a staff member. You get a feeling of stillness, sometimes almost spooky, about the grounds. Nothing seems to be moving. Six buildings lie outside the quadrangle, all of them single-story brick—the three dorms, the cafeteria, the administration building, and the assembly hall. No one sits on, or cuts across, the grass inside the quadrangle. I would guess that's a rule.

Tomorrow I will start group therapy. I won't take part in avocational classes until Monday. They are required two afternoons a week, and a patient can go more often if he wishes. I will have a choice of painting, woodwork, pottery, polishing stones, metalwork, or making woodcuts. I'm considering pottery, which I've never done, but Tip Watson said, "You going to work in the *mud?* Last time I was here, I worked in the mud and my hands broke all out. Shoot some basketball with me, if the [Tip says "the" for "they"] will let us."

Friday

><

Each new patient is given a printed schedule, which we live by Monday through Friday, and it is a full one:

7:00 A.M.   Awakening of patients. (This is no problem because many patients are up and about by six o'clock, some as early as three-thirty and four. Alcoholics often don't sleep well.) Clean bedroom and prepare for breakfast. (We have other chores, too, divided among us, such as sweeping the halls and lobby, polishing the drinking fountains, dusting the furniture, carrying out trash, and taking part in a mass clean-up on Saturday morning, which includes washing the big windows in the front of our dorm.)

7:45   Medicine call. (Each of us is required to take vitamin pills for the first two weeks. Patients who are

22

in bad shape—the most common afflictions seem to be "nerves," sleeplessness, and high blood pressure—may get medication several times a day.)

8:00 Breakfast. (All meals are big and high in calories, except those for patients who are put on special diets. Many alcoholics are undernourished because they quit eating when they start drinking. A taxi driver in our dorm consistently would drop from 200 pounds to 150, at which point he usually would become so sick that he had to enter a hospital. The point, then, is to put weight on the patients. Fortunately, or unfortunately, I don't need any. I came here weighing 215, wanting to weigh 190, and after three days weighed 221. We line up to have our weights recorded each Friday after dinner.)

8:45 Dorm meeting. (Patients elect a dorm leader and he presides over this meeting. It is attended by patients and staff members, offering an opportunity for suggestions, announcements, and complaints—from either side. Charley, the bus driver, is sorely troubled; he wishes patients would assemble properly outside the dorm and have their names checked off his list before riding anywhere with him. Two attendants, sometimes three and four, are always on duty in the dorm, and they come out of their glassed-off office to attend the meeting. Staff members come, too—some mornings Warren Bush, the chaplain; William Lathan, the ARC business manager; and always Nancy Laidlaw, a great-looking psychologist. She is an early-morning pleasure, striding down the long white walk in a splendid, different miniskirt each day, first in the distance, drawing closer, delighting the men, irking the women.)

9:00 Sick call and free time. (Patients who have no need of a doctor can do as they please. The card game "rook" is a chief diversion, but there is the choice of watching television, writing letters, or sitting in front of the dorm and talking.)

9:30–10:15 All patients meet in the assembly room for movie, lecture, or discussion of various aspects of alcohol.

10:15–10:30 Free time.

10:30–11:30 Group therapy with group leader. (Normally, we have five to seven patients in a group, but the number varies as old patients depart and new patients arrive.)

11:45 Medicine call.

NOON Lunch.

1:00–4:15 Avocational classes and/or group therapy as scheduled.

5:00 Supper. (The fish tonight—I don't know what kind—was a rough number. Tip Watson said it was shark and that Friday night always will stand out as the only unpalatable meal of the week.)

6:00 Medicine call (for those who need medication).

6:00 Recreation. See bulletin board for notice of activities. Free time. (Musical groups, most of the time guitar pickers and country singers, come on Thursday evenings; fishing trips are made to nearby lakes and rivers on Friday afternoons.)

10:00 Medicine call.

11:00 Lights out. Bedtime. (Actually, we stay up through TV's eleven o'clock news, Sunday through Thursday. On Friday and Saturday nights patients can watch the "Late Show," which ends about one-thirty.)

We may have visitors from one to four P.M. on Saturday and Sunday. Attendance is compulsory at meetings arranged each Friday evening by Alcoholics Anonymous.

I went to my first group therapy session this morning. Tip Watson and Paul Evans, who came the same day I did, are in the group, too. So is Mr. Wellington, the boy scout leader. Right now we're in with old patients, who will be leaving soon, and we'll be getting newcomers. Today's session, spent mostly getting settled in, didn't especially impress or distress me. I don't know how I will feel sitting with a half-dozen people listening to what's bothering them and telling them what's bothering me, if that is what we are to do. Weldon Bayliss, a big-boned minister who is about six-feet-two, is my group leader. He's at ARC training to be a counselor. I would prefer he weren't training on me—and I would rather have Nancy Laidlaw, the psychologist, instead of a preacher. But I don't want to hurt his feelings by asking to be transferred and he may turn out all right, anyway. Some of his work this morning, though, appeared a little too bookish: "Mr. Relman, you're sitting there with your hands folded across your stomach. Locking in your resentment?"

Patients who wanted to fish this afternoon were taken by bus to a nearby river (they didn't catch anything), but I couldn't go because I haven't been here seven nights—a rule. Tip Watson and I sat on the benches in the sunshine with several old hands who hadn't wanted to go fishing. Tip knew them from previous trips here and to the Big Top. We can see the great green roof of the hospital from our benches. The old-timers seemed pleased to see Tip again.

"Boys, I tell you," he said, "I'm glad to be away from the crazy people. You don't get the same bed two nights in a row. The [they] get in your bed. You take what's open. And the run up and take food right off your tray. Godamighty."

Tip got up from the bench, seeming about to leave, but he took just a few steps and turned, facing us. "Yes, sir," he said, "living in the Big Top is something else." Tip does that often: when he's seated, he gets up; when he's walking, he stops. It takes you fifteen to twenty minutes to go around the quadrangle with Tip. He stops to speak to other patients, practically all he meets, and he stops when you are alone, too, turning, facing you, telling you a particular part of a story that he must enjoy.

Tip is forty-one, a large man with curly black hair, who works now for a company that rents tables, chairs, and party equipment. But he wears faded, unironed cotton shirts, often checks and plaids, that remind you of a small boy. He walks with a limp, ever so slight, that was caused by frostbite when he feel asleep, drunk, in the back of a truck on a January night. I believe I will enjoy Tip. He has great humor and timing. He never ruins a story by indicating that it will be funny, or by laughing in the middle of it. You see only the beginning of a smile that never gets much bigger. For years he was a house roofer. "I could drink all night," he said, "and get out the next morning and get right up on a roof. At least I used to could. Then I got where I didn't like to be up there. Way up there in the air."

Mr. Leland, who shakes and mumbles, was sitting on a bench with us. This morning at breakfast I saw another patient hold coffee to Mr. Leland's lips because he couldn't do it himself. He looked a little steadier this afternoon, but not much. "I just get in my boat," he said, "and go across the river and get one." ("One" is a half-gallon fruit jar of white whiskey that he buys from a bootlegger on the other side of the river.) Once in a bad siege of weather, he said, the river froze too thick for his boat and too thin for him to walk on. "Had to walk seven miles in the snow to get one. Don't believe I could do that any more."

Tip grew up on a small farm and he enjoys talking about his childhood. "We had this pet goat and he would run after my baby sister. When she stopped by a bench, he'd jump up on the bench. When she stopped by the doghouse, he'd jump up on the doghouse. One day she stopped by the well . . ." Tip paused. "There he goes—straight down the well. We got a plow line out of the barn and tied a rake to it and when his head come up we hooked him under the collar and drug him up. That sumbitch spit ten gallons of water and he didn't never jump up on nothing any more."

Tip told of learning to make whiskey when he was fourteen and selling it to sawmill workers. "I built a still down in our bottomland. The first day it got to popping and jumping, making so much fuss I knew my daddy was going to hear it and come down there and beat hell out of me. I threw branches and gunnysacks over it, but it still sounded like a shotgun going off."

"Godamighty, you had too much fire," a man named Mr. Early said. "You got to pull fire when that happens. Wonder it didn't blow your ass off."

"Sure is," Mr. Leland said.

I went tonight to an Alcoholics Anonymous meeting, walking from our dorm to the assembly room with Johnny Ross, a young black man who arrived yesterday. In appearance, Johnny easily is our best-looking patient—gold cuff links, white shirt, good slacks, black-and-white wing-tip shoes—but his nerves are bad and he's moody. "Damn if I'm going to stay here long," he said. Just as Tommy Morgan had taken me to my first lunch, I took Johnny to his, but he couldn't eat. He had a glass of iced tea and a half-slice of bread.

The AA speaker, from another town, was convincing as he told of his downfall and sincere as he described how he now had gone two years without drinking. But he talked too long. I can't stand speakers who talk too long and I don't like meetings in general. My first thought would be that I won't attend AA meetings when I leave here. But a counselor told me something that might make me reconsider. Discussing my chances of quitting drinking, he put it this way: of three patients who leave Butner, *two* fail and must return. A patient's chances of success increase sharply, he said, if he becomes actively involved with AA after leaving here. I surely will think about that.

Saturday

〉✕〈

I WORKED ON A NEWSPAPER ONCE WITH A MAN WHO had quit drinking many years before and he always seemed too cautious and conservative. He was good at his work, but he checked constantly to make sure that his superiors were pleased. Although he had a good sense of humor, he rarely joked about anything "dangerous," especially the newspaper and its owners.

He didn't know it and I didn't know it at the time, but for some reason he was becoming my idea of what a reformed drunk was like. Long before I thought of trying to stop drinking, that image was fixed in my mind, and it came with me to Butner. I wanted to quit drinking, but not at the cost of becoming a eunuch.

Today, waiting for my first visitors, I wondered how I would feel and what I would seem like to them.

A *Farewell to Alcohol*

Bill Ray, a photographer I have known since the late 1940s, called last night and asked if he could drive from Winston-Salem this afternoon to visit. My sister called about noon and said she and my brother-in-law were in Raleigh attending a swimming meet and might be able to visit.

Bill Ray rode up in his white Jaguar, attracting the attention of patients who like automobiles, and he had brought Ed Friedenberg, a news editor whom I have always called "Sam." The time I have spent with both of them, working and drinking, goes back a long way. Bill Ray and I used to ride with federal men and State Highway Patrolmen, chasing the souped-up 1940 and 1950 Fords that screamed out of Wilkes County, North Carolina, carrying white whiskey to the cities. When we caught a load, we would help officers break the half-gallon fruit jars of whiskey, simply by rolling a jar on the ground and throwing another on top of it. Some nights we would roll a few jars out into the darkness and come back later to pick them up for ourselves. I had known Sam even before that, when we were in college. He and I played in the same band, a five-man group that toured the small community after dark, some of us on the hood or fenders of an automobile, making music. He played the violin and I played a Lay's Potato Chips can.

This afternoon, while Bill Ray, Sam, and I were sitting on a bench in front of the dorm drinking grapefruit juice, my sister and brother-in-law came. They all know each other and we talked about old times; new times, too—my being at Butner.

31

"I didn't know whiskey had you so bad, Will," Bill Ray said.

"It had me," I said.

"Well, you drank your share. Enough to retire."

"Honorably," Sam said.

I showed them the dorm and we walked around the grounds, talking, enjoying each other, the first time the five of us had been together in years.

"It's a nice place," my brother-in-law said. "Do you have to drink much to get in here?"

"More than you do," I said. "But you could practice and work up to it."

At four o'clock they left. It had been one of the most pleasant afternoons I've spent in a long while.

For most patients, weekends are the toughest. There are no lectures, films, activities, or group therapy sessions to break the long pull between sunrise and bedtime. Three trips to the cafeteria and endless circling of the quadrangle make up Saturday. Sunday is a repeat. Patients who have visitors are cheered; those who have none are lonely.

If the center has a glaring fault, it is the lack of recreation. Men and women occasionally pitch horseshoes, off near the edge of the woods beside A Dorm, but there is nothing else to do on the grounds except walk and talk. Inside, it's read, write, watch television, or play the card game "rook."

Shuffleboard, badminton, a pool table, a tennis court,

a swimming pool—any of those would be wonderful to have.

You hear so much about "Dr. D" or "Durocher" (Dr. Norman A. Desrosiers, the ARC director) that I wondered if he had some special hard-head philosophy that he had worked out. Something like Spartan living being good for self-indulgent alcoholics. Desrosiers is no ordinary man and it struck me that he might have worked out something, even if it was wrong. He built an airplane and flies it; he built an organ, composes music and plays it; he has been a theologian, a practicing physician and a psychiatrist; he has designed his own house and is building it. On benches in front of the dorm, you hear his name often: "Jackson wouldn't go to rec today—Durocher'll throw his ass in the Big Top."

—"Durocher hates alcohol and he hates people who drink it."

—"When you hear Durocher's liver lecture, you won't ever eat liver again. He brings one right in there in a sack, makes you look at it."

—"Dr. D is a genius."

—"Durocher is pretty handy with his fists, too."

I once asked Dr. Desrosiers if he had some Spartan ideas about recreation. He smiled. "Oh, no," he said. "I'd love to have a gym here and tennis courts. We already have plans to put a gym over near A Dorm. I asked the legislature for money, but we didn't get it." He paused. "But we will."

Sunday

⋈

I N THE COURSE OF A DAY, ESPECIALLY A SUNDAY WHEN
there's nothing to do, you learn a lot about the men
and women around you.

I talked for a long while after breakfast with Julie
Ryan, sitting on a bench in the sunshine. Julie is a
nice-looking woman, slender, in her mid-thirties, I
would guess. If any of us look out of place here, it is
Julie especially. Always she is perfectly groomed, her
black hair in precise place, her bright dresses without
a wrinkle on the hottest days, looking as if she had
just left a Parent-Teacher Association meeting or a
high school play in a small town. But there is an
unhappiness, I think, seldom spoken up, that shows
in the tautness of her face. She has twice tried to
commit suicide, but I didn't ask—and don't know
—how serious she was in her attempts. She is married

34

to a business executive, and he doesn't sound like a man I would enjoy being around. "Our car doesn't stop running when you turn it off," she said. "It's maddening. But Skip won't let me have it fixed. He says he's getting the best gas mileage he ever has and he's not going to let anyone fool with the timing."

Julie has been at ARC once before. After she got out, she didn't drink for three years, then decided to have cocktails on two evenings that she and her husband were visiting friends in Boston. She realized that would cause her to start drinking heavily again, she said, but she did it anyway. When they returned to North Carolina, she began drinking steadily, trying to remain sober only a few days a week—one of them the day of her daughter's ballet lesson.

Julie has had some psychotherapy, but I don't know how much. Enough to speak of "guilt" and "repression." She hopes to get in the same therapy group I'm in, the one Weldon Bayliss leads, and she would be a good addition because some of the men don't look as if they will talk much.

Tip Watson was approaching and I hesitated before calling him over. He knows a lot about machinery and I wanted Julie to tell him about the automobile. But Tip had heard of Julie's suicide attempts and that had puzzled and bothered him. "I guess she's all right," he had said, "but damn if I want to talk to anybody who tries to kill theyself."

Now Tip listened, nodding, as she told him about the automobile. "He's not saving gas," he said. "He's wasting gas. Your husband is crazy as hell, that's all."

Julie said her husband was coming to visit in the afternoon. Tip said he thought he would make a point of it to speak to him about the car.

Johnny Ross, the black man with the bad nerves, was sitting by himself on cement steps at the back of the cafeteria. "Let's go talk to him," I said to Tip. Tip nodded. "We ought to. That doesn't look good—sitting by hisself." Johnny and I have started jogging together; neither of us likes it, but it's the only exercise we get, and company helps. We're running-walking the quadrangle four times each evening, and hope to work up to eight—two miles. As Tip and I passed the dorm, he paused beside Mr. Leland. "Let's go across the river, Mr. Leland," he said, "and *get* one."

Johnny Ross is moody. He was assistant manager of a supermarket and he says he did most of the manager's work, too. "He had a girl friend and he would just take off and leave me. I'd be paying bills and sending stuff to the home office and helping customers, all at the same time." He said he worked swiftly and well when he was drinking because whiskey helped him stay calm with customers who annoyed him. On weekends he would buy eight pints of Scotch for his days off.

As we talked, he seemed homesick for his wife and children and mother. "I don't have to stay in this damn place," he said. "I'm going home." We urged him to give it a couple more days.

"I'm all right now," he said. "I'm not going to drink alkyhol [the pronunciation used by many patients] any more."

"The done a hell of a job curing you," Tip said. "You come in here shaking and three days later you cured."

Johnny said he wouldn't go home today but he was going to speak to Bayliss next week about leaving.

Tip and I went to the parking lot and stayed awhile, directing visitors to the dorms. "You reckon the think we work here?" Tip asked. "Or think we're drunks?" "We look like staff," I said. We walked around the quadrangle again, giving Tip a chance to speak to many of the patients, which he enjoys doing. "Hello, Rooster," he said. Tip speaks kindly to almost everyone, but he doesn't care for the man he calls "Rooster." One night in the dorm Rooster had told Tip of his experiences in Florida. He was broke and drunk and the Salvation Army gave him food and a place to stay. In return, he was driving a truck, picking up donations. "I'd carry most of it in," he said. "But I kept some of the good stuff. I got a TV set." Tip said, "Rooster is one of the sorriest men I've ever seen."

"Rooster" is the only one here that Tip doesn't like. (He seems to feel all right now about Julie Ryan.) Coley Thompson, Tip's roommate, says he had 92 percent of his stomach removed and he talks about it often, sometimes even at meals, but Tip says, "Aw, Coley can't help it."

Mr. Wellington was walking with a man who once was a private pilot for a multimillionaire. "Hello, Pilot," Tip said. "Hello, Mr. Wellington."

Mr. Wellington has a horseshoe of silver hair and a pinkish face; he's a gentle-seeming man. He said he had been fired after working forty-three years for the same company. Unlike many alcoholics who blame bosses for their difficulties, Mr. Wellington says the fault was his. "I was what you call a secret drinker," he said. "I thought no one knew. I would just drink beer at night, but I was making mistakes the next day and I didn't know I was making them. They fired me."

In the afternoon Julie introduced us to Skip, her husband. Tip, smiling, said, "Why don't you get that damn car fixed?" Skip didn't answer.

Tomorrow I'll start avocational classes, which everyone refers to as "recreation." I've seen some good work in the dorm—a couple nice woodcuts, a birdhouse that a man built, several pendants, and a big oil done by Tommy Morgan, the ex-college student, who is going home in a few days. I would like to paint that well, but I'm leaning more toward pottery or woodcuts.

Monday

✖

We ASSEMBLED IN FRONT OF THE DORM AND WATCHED Charley, the bus driver, dressed in white pants and white shirt, hurry down the walk toward us. He got a list from the attendant on duty, showing which of us were to attend recreation. Half of us go on Monday and Wednesday, the other half on Tuesday and Thursday.

Fretting, checking the list, Charley called out the names, "Ross . . . Ryan . . . Watson" . . . and we left, individually, walking 150 yards to the blue bus parked at the rear of the cafeteria. When we were all in the bus, Charley looked the group over several times and began backing out. He looks in the rear-view mirror so often, or turns to look at his charges, that Tip Watson said he believed it would be easier if Charley backed the bus over to the recreation hall, which was an old army building.

Tip and I were sitting near the front. "Where's Galloway?" Tip asked, loud enough for Charley to hear.

"He's in the back," I said.

Charley stopped the bus. "Galloway isn't on here," he said. He studied the list. "Galloway isn't Monday and Wednesday."

"I thought he was going special today," Tip said.

Charley studied the list again. "He's not on here." He looked over the passengers, and the bus began to roll, Charley looking worried.

"Charley ain't going to lose a prisoner," Tip said.

The rec building is crowded and cluttered, but a lot of work gets done. A single room, partitioned off, holds the painters and woodcutters; other sections are for pottery, metalwork, woodwork, and stone-polishing. Behind the building is a basketball hoop. Inside, two bags of golf clubs lean against a wall in the art room.

Tip has changed his mind, for the time being at least, about shooting basketball. He had seen Tommy Morgan's big oil—it is of a desolate farmhouse with a sign in the yard that reads "Condemned"—and admired it. He had even been over here with Tommy to select a large canvas for himself. Perhaps jokingly, perhaps not, he said he had never seen a good painting of a whiskey still and he thought he would do one. Have woods and a stream, he said, with a pickup truck backed up to the site with bags of sugar on it. And maybe a figure or two around the still, he said, if they weren't too hard to draw. Tommy cautioned him against trying to put too much in.

I will be working in the same room with Tip because I have decided to do a woodcut. I liked some that I saw around the dorm. Julie Ryan is going to do woodcuts, too.

Pat Carroll, a pleasant young artist who is a part-time instructor at ARC, showed us where the supplies were and told us to sit down and sketch out an original idea. She would be looking in to comment and advise.

Julie went quickly to doing mushrooms. Her lines, like her own appearance, were precise and clean. Tip was having trouble getting the still going, and I began work, slowly, on a long fishing pier, with ocean, sky, and sand. Vague figures were to be at the end of the pier, holding great sea rods, casting into the ocean.

Mrs. Carroll didn't have to work much with Julie. "Very nice," she said.

She spoke several times with Tip and came to help me. "That's more ambitious than most of our woodcuts," she said. "But I'm pleased if you want to do it." I told her I really would like to do the fishing pier, and she showed me how to make it look as if the pier left the sand and extended out into the ocean. I was having trouble, too, with the figures. She whipped off a series of joined circles—one for a head, one for a torso, four for legs, four for arms. "That's a good way to do it," she said. "Then put the clothes on."

Tip was beginning to wander around. When I went for a drink of water, a member of the recreation staff nodded toward Tip. "He never finishes anything," he said.

Tip had told me about a number of projects that his father had undertaken when Tip was a boy on the farm. "He built a submarine once," Tip said, "and got it in the river. Almost drowned. Another time he decided to build an airplane and he got a big old Hudson engine but his wings were too heavy. It would've taken six Hudson engines to fly it. He put bales of hay on a hill, got on another little rise and revved it up, figuring he'd fly to the hay bales and they'd stop him. He never got off the ground but he got going damn fast down that hill. He missed the hay bales and it like to killed him."

I wondered if Tip's never finishing anything was tied up somehow to his father's submarine and airplane.

I returned to my sketch of the pier, which I hope eventually to turn into a woodcut. As the afternoon wore on, four men—two black, two white—stopped by occasionally to help. One was Tip, who said, "You got to put in more pilings." Mrs. Carroll showed me how to get my fishing lines into the water and out of the sand, where I had my people casting them. I felt I had come a long way since my sixth-grade days when Miss Henderson used to smack me on my right hand because my Christmas tree didn't look like everyone else's.

We saw what I thought was a bad movie today. The hero and his wife lived in a pleasant community and he was a rising young executive. She seemed to like him all right but she wanted fur coats and fine dresses. The bills piled up, but he never said anything; just worried about them at night.

He drank some at home, a little more each night, then he took off for Chicago. He got falling-down drunk in a dive, rolled in an alley, and showed up a night or so later, bearded, clothes askew, at a mission. He had to hear a sermon before he could get anything to eat, and he did. A few lights of revelation showed on his face, and he went down front and was converted.

He stayed at the mission a couple weeks, helping out and distributing pamphlets on the street. Back home, his wife was worried and wondered where he was. He came to like a particular verse in Isaiah, and when he decided to go home he bought a Bible for his wife.

She met him at the door, hugged him, and he brought out the present. Wrapped as it was, it could have been a handbag or a jewel box. She didn't seem excited when she found out it was a Bible and he read the verse from Isaiah. Not mad, but not happy, either, she tossed the Bible aside; it landed still open to Isaiah.

Disappointed, he ran out into the night, got to the downtown section and came to a place with red neon lights that flicked off and on, spelling "BEER." He started to walk on but hesitated. He started again to walk on but hesitated.

She awoke in a great rainstorm, went to the living room and found the Bible open to Isaiah. She read the verse, pulled on a raincoat, ran out into the night, and found him still hesitating at the beer place.

They embraced and started home.

"Any comments?" asked the counselor who had shown the film. We were all together in the assembly hall, the men and women from the three dorms and the men from D Dorm at the Big Top.

No one said anything.

"It all seemed a little fast to me," I said. "Came out too neat."

A man from the Big Top, sitting in the second row, said, "We got to get back to God. We came from God, we got to get back to God."

"That's right," someone said.

"I thought it told the story quite well," said a man from A Dorm.

Fortunately, at least in my view, the ARC was only testing the film. It isn't a part of the program and was being shown to get patients' reactions. Despite the favorable comments, I don't think the film will be put into the program. Aside from being permitted to attend Sunday morning church services and hearing brief references to "God as we understood Him" at AA meetings on Friday night, we do not deal in religion. At least not as a group. If someone wants to talk with Warren Bush, the chaplain, he can—and Warren Bush is a pleasant, easy man to talk with.

When you compare today's quick-save film with others used in our program, especially those made in Canada, a country that appears to know a lot about alcoholism—well, there is no comparison. The Canadian films—and, in fairness, some American films, too —project no easy cures. A line that sticks in my mind came in a scene where a doctor was talking with the wife of an alcoholic: "No, he can't ever drink again. Not *ever*. Not a glass of sherry at Christmastime."

Pondering that thought, I find it fascinating. I don't want a drink right now and I hope I never will. But I have had so many drinks, under such varied circumstances, that drinking is almost as natural to me as putting on my pants to go to work. I am trying to absorb everything that I am told here, so I accept what the doctor said. Certainly I can accept it intellectually and I hope emotionally, too: not a glass of sherry at Christmastime.

Tuesday

×

How did I become an alcoholic? Why did I need to drink? If I quit, will I be happy with my life? (The suicide rate of "recovered alcoholics" is five times greater than that of the general population, meaning that many who quit drinking still are not happy.) After drinking for twenty-seven years, if I stop, what will I seem like to myself and to others?

It's important that I find answers to those questions, at least partial answers, and I spend much of each day reflecting. In arriving at conclusions, I am helped by a number of persons, including Nancy Laidlaw, Weldon Bayliss, and Dr. Desrosiers. He is a man with impressive credentials, and I give weight to what he says.

One of the things he says goes to the core of the ARC philosophy: "We're not drying out drunks here.

We're treating persons who are using alcohol as a coping mechanism. We must treat the emotional needs." It's his contention that the majority of Americans who drink are trying themselves to treat emotional needs, using alcohol as a handy drug to deal with anxiety, tension, fear, grief, depression, frustration, and inhibition. "The term 'social drinker' is meaningless," he says. "If it has any validity at all, it describes a minority of the people who use alcohol strictly at social functions and at social functions alone. And in minimal amounts of one to two drinks." Statistics on drinking vary, but these rounded-off figures will serve: ninety million American adults drink; of these, ten million are alcoholics or bad-problem drinkers; that leaves eighty million who might be considered social drinkers. That's the figure Dr. Desrosiers won't accept. "It is far more likely that the majority of persons who are not yet what we call alcoholic, but who drink, are in reality not *true* social drinkers, but rather persons who use alcohol to treat their underlying emotional disorders. It is this population from which the alcoholic population is drawn, and who constitute a vast body of persons who adjust to life with the aid of chemical means."

I will accept that—whether or not my friends will (about me or about themselves)—and put myself in that group. Certainly I was using "chemical means" to adjust to life. I would not, of course, have put up with that kind of pseudo-psychological junk-talk for a minute if an employer or a fellow next to me in a bar had made the point.

I talked for two hours today with Dr. Desrosiers about drinking—the problem in general, not just my own. When you've been here awhile, listening to all the stories about Dr. Desrosiers building airplanes, composing music, and all the other things he can do, you begin to think Leonardo da Vinci has parachuted into our pinewoods. Well, if Desrosiers comes up a little short, it's not enough to worry about—he is quite some figure to have here. The feeling you get most about him is one of quickness, both mental and physical; that and a vague instinct that you would not cross him lightly, although he is not a big man. Talking with you, he is gracious and smiling, moving across biology and pathology, into psychology and theology, picking up philosophy and psychiatry, sweeping you along with him—*hell, you and I know these things*—enjoying, I am sure, the legend that has built up around him, this genius of the pinewoods. He is forty-seven, a native of Rhode Island who came to the South during World War II, studied at Duke in the wartime V-12 program, and never left.

The point Dr. Desrosiers puts the greatest stress on is the necessity of an alcoholic's learning new ways of behavior. Simply not drinking is not enough. The ARC looks on abstention as a minimum requirement. "Suppose a person stops drinking," Dr. Desrosiers said, "but doesn't learn a new way of dealing with life? All of his problems are still there." That's when he told me about the suicide rate of recovered alcoholics.

What is the danger signal for a drinker?

"Any time he feels the *need* for a drink. Say, a minister to go into his pulpit to deliver a sermon—and we've had ministers here."

But doesn't almost everyone, after the initial experimenting, feel the *need*?

"Well, yes. The danger comes much sooner than is realized."

If a person is drinking heavily and realizes he has a problem, what's the best thing to do?

"Usually he can find someone in the community—a pastor or mental health people—to talk to. He needs to sit and talk, find out what's behind his drinking."

When an employer feels a man is drinking too much, what should he do?

"Confront him directly and warn him. The next time there should be absolute insistence that he see someone for treatment and absolute insistence on sobriety. The third time, fire him. It's not helping a man to do otherwise."

When does brain damage occur?

"It's a biological controversy. Are you familiar with Knisely's work? He believes it happens quickly." Dr. Melvin Knisely, working at the Medical University of South Carolina, has done extensive studies of the blood. Until recently, many physiologists believed that persons did not suffer permanent damage from occasional drinking. Dr. Knisely's work offers strong evidence that this is not true—that even light drinking may kill brain cells. He and two associates studied the capillaries in the retinas of persons who had been drinking. Even in the cases of persons who had drunk as little as one large glass of beer, the doctors detected a "sludging" of the blood, a wadding up in the small arteries of the red cells that produce oxygen. If this same "sludging" occurs in the small arteries of other organs—and extensive tests on rabbits suggest that it does—brain cells supplied by these small arteries can be deprived of oxygen and suffer permanent damage and even cell death.

If a person has been drinking for a long while and quits, can he regain good physical condition?

"Well, it depends upon how long and how much. The human body has great grace and built-in forgiveness. The liver works like hell to cure itself. Also, it is said that we have many, many more brain cells than we ever use. The brain and liver can be damaged and a person can still function, although at a reduced level."

Dr. Desrosiers and I ended our conversation on the point that interests me most—new behavior. "A man has to learn how to live differently," he said. "He must find a creative resolution. He must stop drinking and use his resources."

Wednesday

⋈

I<small>N OUR GROUP THERAPY SESSION THIS MORNING,</small>
Weldon Bayliss went directly to the same point—the
necessity of changing our lives.

Why do you drink? he asked each of us. Why do
you *need* whiskey? Whatever the reasons, he said, we
must identify them, then find new ways to live without drinking.

We sit close together in a group session, a couple
of us on a couch, the rest in chairs ringed about a
small room. "What about you, Mr. Thompson?"
Bayliss asked.

Coley Thompson is extremely nervous. He's in his
forties and hasn't worked for a number of years, following a series of operations that removed much of

his stomach. He's a friendly man, constantly offering something—"If you ever want any cookies or gum, go right in my room"—taking your laundry out of the washer and putting it in the dryer if you're busy, picking up change at the administration building because someone might need it at night to make a phone call from our dorm.

"Well, I just sit there at the house all day," Coley said, "with nothing to do. I get up in the morning and I say I'm not going to drink much beer today. Go down to the store and get maybe three and say that's all I'm going to drink. But I walk back and get a six-pack. Later on I'll go again, and sometimes when Nell [his wife, who works] comes home I'll just be sitting there looking at beer cans all over the room. Don't even bother to pick them up."

"Don't you have any hobbies?" Bayliss asked.

"I like to fish but I can't get there. The state got my driver's license." (A great many patients have lost their driver's licenses.)

"Isn't there something you could do at home?" Julie Ryan asked.

"I like to fix furniture," Coley said. "Chairs, tables. I do that sometimes."

"Why don't you open a small business at home?" Bayliss asked.

"Won't anybody pay you," Coley said. "I've tried it. You get the parts and fix the thing, then they just leave it—never pick it up. They go buy a new chair."

"Well, we've got to find something for you to do

when you go home," Bayliss said. "What about you, Mr. McIlwain?"

"I'm not sure," I said. "I wasn't happy a great deal of the time, but that's not what you're talking about. You're asking me *why*."

"You've got to figure it out," Bayliss said. "What about you, Mr. Ross?"

"I had too much aggravation," Johnny Ross said. "I did *everything* at that store. I'd be sending something to the home office, it's in California, and have to put it down to help a customer. You think people can't worry you? They come in wanting something they heard about on TV—only they can't remember the name. You get something down from the top shelf and they change their minds. All the time the manager off somewhere drinking with his girl. Hell." Johnny paused. "I got to keeping me a fifth of Scotch there. Man, I could sail through the work—paying bills, sending off stuff, helping people, not worrying about anybody. Sail through the work."

I remembered, of course, the years when I could *sail* through the work. "Did it always work?" I asked Johnny Ross.

"It sure did," he said. "I could always do better work when I was drinking."

"Is that really the truth?" Bayliss asked.

"Sure," Johnny Ross said.

"I believe it," I said. "For a while. But finally you get where you can't sail."

"Are you going back to the same job?" Bayliss asked Johnny Ross.

"Too much aggravation," Johnny said. "I'm going to study electronics and go in with my uncle. I'm not going to drink any more alkyhol."

"How do you plan to stop?" Tommy Morgan asked. It was his last day in the group.

Johnny searched for a card in his wallet. "I'm going to call this man. He's in the alkyhol council over there. Last time I was here and went home, he drove me around, letting me help him with the alkyholics. Went to some of the best places in town. He made phone calls about jobs for me. This time I don't drink."

"You're mighty quiet, Mr. Evans," Bayliss said to Paul Evans.

"I'm listening." Paul didn't say anything else.

"Well, you're going home, Mr. Morgan," Bayliss said. "How's it going to be?"

"I hope all right," Tommy said.

"Do you see any problems?"

"I hope not." Tommy usually talks easily. But I had noticed last night and again at breakfast that he was uneasy, perhaps wondering how life would be on the outside.

"You've always thought of yourself as a nice guy, haven't you?" Bayliss asked Tommy. "But wasn't some of that 'nice guy' because you couldn't assert yourself?"

"Yes, sir," Tommy said. "I used to drink beer in this place and a man came in there picking at me for three months. I got madder and madder but I didn't say a thing. Then one day I beat him and stomped him. I thought I was going to stomp him to death."

"We all must learn to express anger," Bayliss said. "If we don't, the anger comes out in some other form. Like depression. Some morning you feel extreme depression and you don't know why . . . but if you think back, you may find that a couple days before you didn't stand up for your rights."

Several of us conceded that we hadn't enjoyed much middle ground—that it was almost always say nothing or fight.

"I know I've been that way," I said. "I let people do things that bothered me and didn't say anything."

"I broke a man's jaw with a hammer once," Coley Thompson said. "Another time I drove my leg through a window." He showed the scars. "I just couldn't say anything when somebody made me mad."

"That's it," Bayliss said. "And you probably wouldn't have anything wrong with your stomach today if you had been able to."

Bayliss told of a time when he was in school and got angry with another fellow. "We agreed to meet at the flagpole and we did. I drew my hand back and I don't remember anything else. When I woke up, I was all by myself. But we were good friends after that."

Bayliss looked at Mr. Wellington, who had been sitting quietly. "You seem like a passive man, Mr. Wellington."

"Well, yes, sir," Mr. Wellington said. "I am."

"Have people been pushing you around all your life, Mr. Wellington?"

"Yes, sir," Mr. Wellington said. "You could say that, yes, sir."

"That's got to stop," Bayliss said. "You've got to quit letting people push you around, Mr. Wellington."

Our hour was running out, and Bayliss said he would see us tomorrow. He might still sound a little too pat, sitting there among us with his earnest answers, big-boned and preacherish, in his narrow neckties and drip-dry slacks—but I am beginning to enjoy him.

As we walked toward the dorm, several of us fell in beside Mr. Wellington. "You've got to meet people at the flagpole, Mr. Wellington," I said.

"You're damn right," Tip Watson said. He stopped in the center of the walk and put his hand on Mr. Wellington's shoulder, studying his benign pink face and horseshoe of silver hair. "Hell, Mr. Wellington, if you got in a good first lick you might whup some of those fellows. I'd go home and settle up some old scores, just like Mr. Bailey [Tip calls him "Bailey"] said." Other group members joined in. That was the birth of Fighting Mr. Wellington, a man who would write home first and give people a choice of leaving town or fighting. The plan, right now, is to have him start on the rich side of town, where residents have been drinking and are out of condition, get a few wins under his belt, and then work his way to Oak Street, a tough street.

A *Farewell to Alcohol*

I thought a lot tonight about Coley Thompson, Tommy Morgan, Fighting Mr. Wellington, and myself. All of us have approached life in much the same manner.

Thursday

✕

I HAVE BEEN AT BUTNER TEN DAYS, BUT IT SEEMS much longer. I can recall only three "new places" in my lifetime that I have felt as sharply: entering elementary school, going to boot camp in the Marine Corps, and moving to New York and *Newsday*.

What do you think it's like being an alcoholic and living with no one but alcoholics? Would you suppose that a dormitory full of drunks (though sober now) would fight? Quarrel? Sulk? Withdraw? What?

It is the most considerate, congenial group that I have ever been a member of. That includes Sunday School classes, football teams, college fraternities, newspaper city rooms, and cocktail parties. Men and women, a few who can't read or write, hold doors open for others to pass through; redneck countrymen sit down at dinner with black men with Afro haircuts, and they talk; patients see a new member coming toward the dorm and they go out to help with the luggage; they help, too, when a patient leaves; constantly they inquire about one another's well-being—"Feeling better this morning, Mr. Leland?"

For all of the formal effort put forth by the staff, there may be equal therapy in our just being together —so many alcoholics studying each other. *That* therapy, which comes at cafeteria tables and on benches in the sunshine, may be as great as the therapy provided by counselors and psychologists. You know that nobody's trying to con you. You're not talking to a doctor who may be trying to scare you about your liver, or a preacher who's moralizing over you. You're talking to a man who's tried it, and if he says its impossible to drink even half a beer unless you want to start all over again—well, if he tells you that, you can believe it. Because he will tell you that he hadn't had a drink for nine months and was convinced that he could drink moderately "like everybody else." He was drunk for three months, went into d.t.'s, got carried to John Umstead Hospital, and now is with us at ARC.

There are other benefits. One is that it's easier to perceive and understand your own flaws and troubles if you slip up on them indirectly—see them first in men and women around you, wonder if yours are similar, and then conclude that they are. You see alcoholics kidding themselves, and realize that you've been doing the same thing. Another benefit is simply that there are horror cases around you. You look each morning at Mr. Leland, mumbling, eye-batting, shaking, and you think: If I don't stop now, I'll get like Mr. Leland.

We talk easily among ourselves because we all have at least one thing in common—the sure knowledge of what it's like to be a drunk. That cuts across all superficial differences. I have had seventeen years of schooling; Mr. Early, the trucker, probably has had two or three, or none. Coley Thompson doesn't work, Tip Watson was a roofer, Mr. Wellington was a white-collar man. But we all are much alike. I thought about that yesterday in Weldon Bayliss' group when we discussed what apparently is a common failing of alcoholics—lack of assertiveness. It shows in many of us. Without getting too psychological, I would make a couple of guesses why. Certainly it comes in part from childhood experiences. But I believe, too, that some of the characteristic can be acquired later. A chronic drunk is vulnerable, always feels in danger— in danger of being caught by a cop, caught by a boss, caught by a wife. This thinking spreads to take in almost everyone an alcoholic encounters—gas-station attendants, grocery clerks, strangers on the streets. If nobody's hassling you, don't look for trouble. Fear builds up in an alcoholic, fear that he has been caught and is about to be pounced on. One night Tommy Morgan, the ex-college boy, who left yesterday, and I were sitting in the lobby talking about that very point. The phone rang and another patient called out that it was for me.

"Mr. McIlwain, this is Sergeant McCarthy at A Dorm . . ." *Damn, who is Sergeant McCarthy? What's he want with me?* "Mr. McIlwain . . ." *That attendant must have told him—she saw me walking with a visitor an hour after visiting hours.* "Mr. McIlwain, I wondered if you had any cuff links. I've got some visitors coming Saturday and I have this nice shirt that . . ." Suddenly I realized who it was: a retired Army sergeant who is a patient in A Dorm; everybody calls him "Sarge."

I went back and told Tommy what had happened. We both laughed, but we knew it wasn't funny. "Are you afraid to answer a phone?" Tommy asked.

"In a way," I said. "Yes, I guess I am."

"I am," Tommy said. "But I hope I'll get where I won't be."

Both physically and mentally I feel better than I have in at least three years. Simply not drinking for a few days helped. Remorse and depression, which had dogged me constantly, eased immediately. I was engaged in an effort to help myself, one that seemed to be working, and that produced a euphoric effect. It put me in a good frame of mind to accept anything that is offered here.

Getting up in the morning has become a great pleasure, and that was not the case before Butner. I awake between six and six-thirty, without being called, and look out to see if it's going to be a pretty day. I look forward to getting to the lobby of our dorm. A great urn of water is kept boiling, day and night, for instant coffee, and milk and six kinds of juice are kept in the refrigerator. I drink coffee and juice and read the Raleigh and Durham morning newspapers.

I don't wake up shaking, sweating, hot and cold, snuffling and disoriented. I don't wake up frightened, groping to put together exactly what I had done the night before. This is common, of course, with alcoholics, and some of them here had a lot worse time than I did. One man said he would get up in the morning and look quickly around the house to see if he had broken anything. Then he would go immediately to the garage and circle his car, studying it, praying not to find that he had hit something or someone the night before.

My own case was never that extreme, but I've been told that it could have become so. I would try to put together minute pieces of conversations—pieces that were of no importance, but the inability to recall them was frightening. It meant, I must have sensed, that sooner or later I would not be able to remember the big things, either.

I'm enjoying thinking while sober. It's like finding a new pleasure. An alcoholic with the slightest degree of introspection wonders all the time—about himself and about others. *Would I have done that if I hadn't been drinking? Would I have done it differently? Better? Am I losing my skills? At least some? If I come down hard on a point, will people say ah, hell, he was drunk? Does anyone know what's happening to me? Does the owner of the newspaper? What does he mean, "How're you this morning, Bill?"*

When I was drinking steadily, I found that ago-

nizing. Now I feel able to consider an event or comment, good or bad, in a clear light.

I have started writing again—pretty well, I believe.
I had been working on a magazine piece before I left
home, and a day's work, spent drinking vodka and
Sprite, had finally got where it would produce a half-
page of copy. If I had been writing sonnets, that might
have been sufficient, but on a 7,000-word magazine
story, it was slow going.

Several other things have happened to me here. On
the fourth or fifth night I shaved off a beard that I
had worn for three years. I gave away a pair of sun-
glasses and didn't bother to get new ones. I didn't
really think about why I did either, but the counselors,
I suppose, might say that I'm coming out of hiding.
Today I was elected dorm leader, and I was moved by
that, pleased that these men and women, all sorts,
want me to represent them. I will do all that I can.
I receive letters from my wife and children, which
makes me feel good and bad at the same time. I will
not go home when I leave here—I'm not sure where
I will go. It is not easy to end a marriage of eighteen
years. One of my daughters wrote to me about the
woodcut that I am working on: "You have always
been good at trying new things. Like the woodcut . . .
and ice-skating, and trying to stop drinking."

Friday

✂

THIS WAS THE DAY THE SPEED MAN CAME, AND I believe we may have a miraculous cure on our hands. He sailed in this afternoon, weighing 126 pounds, walking eighteen inches above the pavement. He said his name was Booker and that he had been on amphetamines for seven years but that he wasn't on them any more. He said he got off them and onto whiskey and that was his downfall, the reason he was ARC. But he said later, early tonight, that he believed he had the whiskey beaten, too, and that he might go home in the morning.

That may be just as well; he certainly spoke highly of speed, and it appeared for a while that he might win some converts. We sat on benches out front, eight or nine of us, and Booker told of the glories. "Boys, there's nothing like it. I did a six-week job on a bank in Wilmington in eleven days. Decorated it. Didn't sleep for eleven days and eleven nights. I just wanted everybody to stand back and let me work. Sensitive? You can hear a pin drop thirty feet up the walk. If you've never made love when you're on speed, well, you've just never made love." His listeners, as if a single man, leaned forward. "Yeah?" Booker was silent a moment. "Yes, sir," he said. "Yes, sir. There was just one thing—I was on it two years . . . before I could do anything." His audience slumped back, and someone said, "The hell with it."

From a distance, something like that might sound silly, of no value. I believe, though, we need a Speed Man to show up now and then as a change of pace. We get our share of films and lectures. So if our "funny" things are silly, grim-silly some of the time, they seem somehow to fit into the program.

Later I asked a truck driver who is a patient in our dorm about Booker's story. He said he didn't understand Booker's romantic problems but that it certainly is true that a person on speed could go on without sleep. Taking "black beauties" or "yellow birds," he said, he used to drive tremendous distances without sleep. "But when you crash [the pills wear off], it's hell."

We had a full schedule today—a good group therapy session in the morning, a fishing trip this afternoon, and an AA meeting tonight.

The therapy session got off to a rough start. Johnny Ross told Weldon Bayliss he wanted to leave ARC. He wanted to go home.

"Then go ahead," Bayliss said. "Leave right now. Go get your things and leave."

Johnny got up and left.

"I don't think you had to be that rough on him," I said. "He might have made you mad, but you could have talked to him."

Bayliss didn't seem to hear; he didn't acknowledge what I had said. For whatever reason, Johnny's wanting to leave had really burned him.

When we got going, I suppose it was on a fitting note—suppression of anger.

Coley Thompson told about his childhood with a tough stepfather. "He would give his own son the good meat," Coley said, "and give me fat. He gave him money for cold drinks but wouldn't give me and my sisters any. He didn't even want my sisters to use electricity to iron their blouses."

"Did you hate him?" Bayliss asked.

"No," Coley said. "I just thought he had bad raising."

"Did you ever speak to him about it?"

"No, I just kept away from him as much as I could."

No one else in the group was talking.

Bayliss went on with the questioning: "Mr. Thompson, what if a man wanted to break in front of you in line in the cafeteria? Would you let him?"

"Yes, sir."

"What if there was only one potato left?"

"Well, I'd fight him." Coley was silent a moment. "No, I'd give him half."

"But what if he wanted the *whole* potato?"

"I'd fight him."

"Is that the only way to live?" Bayliss asked.

"It's how I've been," Coley said.

Several of us acknowledged, as we had at the last session, that we have lived a lot that way—taken too much junk off people without saying anything about it. Certainly the point is sinking into my thinking. I consider often how I have lived and how I plan to live when I leave here. Bayliss puts it well: there are many ways to stand up for your rights without knocking an offender flat on his back. That may seem a curious piece of knowledge for me to be acquiring after forty-five years of living in a reasonably polished environment. But somehow it was rooted in me, I believe, that if a man wanted to avoid violence he didn't take strong exception or raise his voice. I may be manufacturing a heritage that I don't really have, but as a boy and as a newspaper reporter I was around a lot of tough Southerners. The enduring recollection is that not many words were passed between persons in disagreement before one said, "Boy, I'll whup yo ass," and got about it, either succeeding or failing. (My personal favorite is, "Boy, I'll turn yo ass evahway but loose.")

Weldon Bayliss turned to Mr. Wellington. "What are you thinking about, Mr. Wellington?"

"Well, I hope I can get my old job back," Mr. Wellington said. "I think coming here might be a . . . might help cause the company to reconsider me. And this pill . . . I think if I take this pill . . ."

Bayliss said, "Antabuse."

"It might help with the company," Mr. Wellington said.

I decided I would stay after the group session and ask Bayliss if he didn't think he should get Mr. Wellington off his idea of getting his old job back. From talking with him around the dorm, several of us have come to feel that Mr. Wellington wasn't fired just for drinking beer at night. We believe he was in over his head with that particular job; his halting manner makes that seem likely.

"How long did you have the job, Mr. Wellington?" Bayliss asked.

"Well, I was with the company forty-three years," Mr. Wellington said. "I worked on the floor until I got this job in the office two years ago."

"Before you got fired," I said, "had anyone spoken to you about your work?"

"Well, yes," Mr. Wellington said. "About a year ago."

"What did they say?"

"They said well . . . I would have to do better."

"It's a tough time to get a job," Bayliss said. "Do you suppose, Mr. Wellington, that you should consider trying to find another job? Even a lesser job?"

My respect for Bayliss went up right then.

"Well, I'd like to get my old job back," Mr. Wellington said.

At that point Johnny Ross walked in. "They said I couldn't go. There's something on my papers that says I can't go without Dr. Durocher seeing me."

"I see," Bayliss said. "Well, sit down, Mr. Ross."

The session turned to family problems. Paul Evans said he had been separated from his wife for four years and missed his three daughters. "I think they need a father," he said. "But when I was home I'd be drinking and they could tell I wasn't the same. Even the little one could tell."

My children could tell, too, and that realization hurts. For many years I read them novels or short stories at night, or just sat and talked, but in the last year before I came here they had taken to going more directly to their own rooms at night. Politely, after a few words, "Have a good day, Dad?" they went away. I wish I could take back that year and change it, but I can't. I hope that in the rest of my life I won't let whiskey or anything else ruin wonderful things.

Julie Ryan, who sits next to me in group sessions, asked Paul Evans, "Do you think you and your wife can get back together?"

"I don't know," Paul said. "We just couldn't talk. Sometimes when I wasn't even drunk, she'd say, 'I'm not going to talk to you when you're like that.' "

"Are you and your wife together, Mr. Watson?" Bayliss asked.

"No, sir, we've been separated fifteen years," Tip Watson said. "She was an alcoholic. Once when I really tried hard, wasn't drinking and was working every day, I'd come home at night and there wouldn't be any supper. She'd be sitting there drinking. Or sitting there with a woman friend drinking."

Julie Ryan said her husband's drinking bothered

her. "We go to dinner parties and Skip won't accept a drink. 'Oh, no, I'll do anything to help poor Julie'— that's the idea he gives around town. But he wants to keep whiskey at home and drink it. I make him drink in the garage."

"Do you really?" Tip asked.

"Yes, I do. I wouldn't mind if he weren't such a hypocrite about it. 'I'll do anything to help poor Julie.' We've got a lot to work out if we're going to get along together."

Mr. Wellington, Tip, Julie, and I walked back to the dorm together. "Let me feel your arm, Mr. Wellington," Tip said. "You getting in good shape?"

It might seem unkind to joke with Mr. Wellington, but I believe it makes him feel better. Besides his job, he's got a lot on his mind. Walking yesterday, he told me that his wife had been sick recently. As we talked, it developed that she had been in a hospital for over a month, and had been critically ill.

Twenty of us got on the blue recreation bus this afternoon to go fishing at Lightning Lake, a muddy pond nearby. We went through the usual thing with Charley. "Have you lost anybody today, Charley?" He went on checking his list. "Where's Rooster?" Tip asked. Charley looked for Rooster.

Nobody was catching anything, not even getting a bite, and Tip and I walked down into the bushes where Mr. Leland was fishing alone. "Mr. Leland, let's go across the river and *get* one," Tip said. Mr. Leland's cork was bobbing, his cane pole jumping. We threw in beside him and didn't get a nibble. Mr. Leland was still getting all kinds of action. Finally Tip realized why. "Mr. Leland," he said, "you shaking so bad we can't tell what's happening. Can you lay your pole across a branch?" Mr. Leland did, and his cork sat as still as ours.

On the way home, and I don't know why, I suddenly wanted a drink or a cigarette. I haven't smoked in three years. The feeling about the drink didn't seem to spring from my mind; I hadn't been *thinking* about whiskey. It was as if I could taste it in my mouth, that and the taste of a cigarette.

At the AA meeting tonight, the men from D Ward at the Big Top came in whooping and hollering. "The got ahold of something at the hospital," Tip said. He explained that it happened sometimes—patients found alcohol.

Our speaker was a tanned, handsome man who is a dispatcher for a trucking company. "Maybe I can save some of you some time," he said. "If you're wondering whether you'll ever be able to drink again, don't bother. You can't. Do you know what one of the greatest dangers is? You leave here and you get along just fine. I did for three years. You start saying to yourself, 'Maybe I never was an alcoholic after all. I never did drink all that weird stuff that those *real* alcoholics drink.' You think you can drink again —and this time control it. You can't. I tried it."

I believe if I hadn't heard that man tonight, I would have come to feel just as he did—and tried it. Maybe, as he said, he saved me some time.

Saturday

✕

AFTER WE FINISHED CLEANING THE DORM THIS MORN-
ing, I started writing, working on the magazine piece
that had fallen off to a trickle before I came here.
Throughout the day patients stopped by my room to
see me, and a couple times I went out to the benches
for sunshine.

Mr. Early, the trucker, came in and asked if I would
write a letter to his wife. I thought he meant just
type it, but he meant compose it. He told me what
he wanted to say and I wrote the letter, a strange
feeling.

I've talked a lot with Mr. Early. He's a good-
natured man, strong-looking, with a big stomach. Tip
Watson jokes with him at medicine calls. "The giving
you a shrinker pill this morning, Mr. Early? What's
that, Mr. Early, one of those sparklers—I don't

want to see it. Did you sign a paper saying they can give you all those experiment pills?" Mr. Early has started joining in: "I got a yellow and green one." But Tip says, "I don't even want to look at it."

One morning during a hard rain Mr. Early said matter-of-factly that eels fell during rainstorms. One of us said well, we'd heard about frogs . . . "That's right," Mr. Early said. "And snakes and turtles. The sun draws them up and the rain brings them down."

No one makes fun of Mr. Early. He's here for the same reason that Ralph Leonard, the mathematician, is here. And for the same reason that I am here. And Julie Ryan and Jack Durham, a writer. And Tip and Mr. Wellington and Rooster and Mr. Leland. And Luther Moore, a quiet man who works in a factory. Luther is thirty-four, black, the father of six children. During the two days he's been in our therapy group he hasn't said a word. But he's friendly, and I talk with him at meals and on the benches. He said the noise of the machines bothers him and he hopes to get a different job when he goes home.

One of the reasons Butner is interesting is that it gives you an opportunity to be with all sorts of men and women. A private $100-a-day clinic tends to draw patients of much the same economic and social levels. Of course, that may be the very thing some patients want. I believe, too, that they feel they can keep their drinking problem more of a secret by going to a private clinic. I know one man who won't go *anywhere*. He says he's afraid people will find out he's an alcoholic and also that his business will go to pieces

73

while he's away. I think he's overlooking a couple of sure things: if you're an alcoholic, you don't fool many people—they know you've got a great problem. And your business certainly is going to pieces if you don't do something. Finally, I don't mind people knowing I'm at Butner trying to accomplish something, not just sitting at home doing the same old thing, pouring down the vodka.

It may be that the public identifies Butner, the town and the complex of institutions, with the big mental hospital here, the John Umstead Hospital. Tip Watson said to me, "Don't say you're at Butner, say the ARC—people will think you're at the Big Top."

Whatever outsiders think, this strikes me as a good place, worth the trouble to come to. The staff says it's one of the finest programs in the country, and I have no reason to doubt that.

Sunday

><

I HAVE HEARD OF SINGLE INCIDENTS—SOME DRAMATIC, some slight—that convinced a man to stop drinking. But I wonder about those stories. I recall a Southern industrialist, a multimillionaire and member of one of the "finest old families," who had been drinking for years. His conviction to stop, as it was described to me, came on a weekend several years ago: "His daughter had weekend guests in their home . . . five or six girls from school . . . and Mayland [not his real name] came down to the living room to talk with them. He vomited in the middle of the rug and passed out on the floor—right in front of his daughter and her friends. Mayland hasn't had a drink since."

And I've heard of a single force—love or fear: "Vicki told him she would leave him. The very next time he got drunk, she said, she would leave and never come back. Jack quit on the spot."

Those things may happen, sunbursts of motivation that strike a person. But more often, I think, he's moved by a combination of reasons, ones that have been creeping into his mind for months, perhaps years. Surely that was the case with me. You can't scare a drunk into quitting—he knows he might get fired, but that by itself won't stop him. And you can't beg him—*please, do try for everyone's sake*. And you can't shame him—*you made an absolute fool of yourself*.

No. He's heard that before.

But if a man's lucky, many things come together for him, seeming to form a single thread, and he decides to quit drinking. Or try, at least. The coming together for me, I believe, was a fluke, a shot in the night that hit something. I set out to romance a nineteen-year-old college girl—what are the chances of anything substantial coming of that?—and wound up thinking that I might be able to change my whole life. Many things, none of them good, were happening to me at the time. I was depressed and ashamed of my lack of accomplishments, yet unable to do anything worthwhile that would help me shake those feelings. My interest in almost everything was gone. Besides my three children, tennis was the only thing that I still enjoyed. For a while I managed not to drink in the mornings in order to be sober, even if hung over, when I played at noon. But I finally gave up that effort, too. I didn't enjoy reading newspapers, talking to people, listening to music, or going anywhere. That was a terrible feeling because I was almost convinced that my interest would not come back. If that were true, I not only would never be happy, I wouldn't be able to earn a living. Although I never told anyone, I felt that I might not be able ever to work on a newspaper again.

It was with all those feelings of despair—and with considerable lust—that I stalked Lee, beautiful, long-legged, golden, a girl who had been a junior tennis champion and first academically in a high school graduating class of 429. The few people who knew of my undertaking thought I finally had gone crazy. A fat, bald, old man, now depraved and sick. It was mostly a blur to me. But when I wasn't at just the right level of drunkenness, I would worry some myself about being fat and bald and old, having those handi-caps in trying to trap a golden girl. We played tennis, drank beer, and listened to rock musicians I had never heard of. We talked very little. Well, actually I talked all the time, but she rarely said much. Even when I was very drunk, I sometimes would see my pursuit of Lee in a light that most probably was accurate—I was trying desperately to save what little I had left by clutching at her perfect youth. But whatever the reason, however futile my effort might be, I was *interested* in something again—if only in drunkenly planned logistics of how to stalk her effec-tively.

Around that interest, many hopes began to coalesce. They seemed at first just drunken thoughts to make myself feel better, but soon I began to believe them: I would run two miles at night on the university track and become fit again; I would remain sober in the mornings so that I could listen more carefully to what little she said; I would love her and make her happy and be happy myself; I would become honest again and worthwhile and quit being afraid; I would stop writing a superficial novel about Bill Moyers and write a better one; I would return to the newspaper business, and even if I never got to the top again, I would be better than I had ever been; I would start my life all over again with her and I would do all of those things.

I told Lee practically none of that. And sitting in my office in the Wake Forest library, drinking vodka and Sprite each day, I seemed not on my way toward accomplishing those things, either. I did tell her that I was in worse shape than she thought and that I should go to Butner. "Why don't you just quit drinking by yourself?" she asked. I told her I didn't think I could. "I don't see why not," she said. "But if you think you should go, then go."

This afternoon, a warm, bright Sunday, I sat on a bench under the oak trees and waited for Lee to come to Butner. It would be the first time she had seen me since I came here.

I sat, waiting, and I thought about many things. I thought what a flimsy reed it was for a man to build his life on—the belief that he could accomplish all of these things because of a girl. But I thought, too, that I would take any reed I could lay my hands on; it might even work.

I have talked with Dr. Desrosiers about motivation,

how much does a man have to have, where does it come from, and what can the ARC do to turn a life around. He told me many things that I already knew: that to quit drinking, a man had to come here with strong motivation; he might have found that motivation in any number of ways—suffering too much pain, having a clear realization of how shoddy a person he had become, a sorting out of religious and philosophical beliefs of what a man's life should be, being inspired by someone or some thing and wanting to emulate what he had witnessed. Most of the ARC's approach, he said, is based on an educational process. "If we can show you where you've gone wrong and some of the reasons why and also demonstrate a better and more successful way of doing things, then it might work. That is, if your old habit patterns aren't all encompassing. Established habits and ways of doing things are not easily broken. It takes one hell of a lot of successes in new behavior to overcome old ways of living."

It was one-thirty and Lee, who was driving a borrowed car, would be here soon. I was nervous and concerned. I had been all morning, even since yesterday afternoon, but it was growing stronger now. What would I seem like to her? And what would Butner and the patients seem like to her? I had grown accustomed to them—Mr. Leland, mumbling, shuffling, his zipper half open; Tip Watson, funny, charming, but looking defeated, too, his face old for forty-one, a slight limp from frostbite when he had fallen asleep, drunk, in the back of a truck on a January night;

Mr. Wellington, a cultured, gentle man who you knew, by looking at him, was broken and could never cut it again in business. However ragged and erratic my behavior at Wake Forest had been, Lee, I thought, had never seen me in a light of ruin and failure. Would she now, looking at these men with whom I had a common bond, all of us being alcoholics? My hold on her was at best tenuous, and this might snap it, scaring hell out of a kid who had never seen such failure and despair.

She came, driving fast, sliding on the gravel in the parking lot, her blond hair blowing in the open window, and I was all the more afraid. I didn't even try to be funny or make jokes about the place; we just started walking around the quadrangle, not saying much as I pointed out the buildings where I eat, sleep, and go to group therapy. "It certainly is quiet here," she said. "It's almost spooky." I told her that on weekdays more people moved around, but she was right, it was a quiet place. "Why don't people sit on the grass?" she asked. "I think it's a rule," I said.

As we approached C Dorm, I could see several patients sitting on benches, and I decided that we should stop and speak to them. It wasn't particularly a thought-out decision; I suppose I just saw no way to escape it: if she was going to be frightened off by my being here with these men and women, it might as well happen right now. I introduced her to Julie Ryan, Mr. Leland, and Tip Watson. "Hi," she said. Mr. Leland said something I couldn't understand, and Tip smiled, looking at her. "You play tennis with him?

I 'magine you beat him pretty good." "Yes." Tip, still smiling at her, said, "I figured you could." Julie Ryan, who always looks good, said, "Isn't it a pretty day?"

We moved on, still circling the quadrangle, and I said, "I like Tip a lot." "He seems like a neat guy," Lee said. We sat in the entrance of the administration building, closed on Sunday, and talked until it was time for her to go. "I'm glad you like it here," she said. "I won't be able to come again before you get out, but I'll write. Call me."

I watched her drive away, fast, as she always drives, and I went on planning our lives.

Monday

⋈

IN TWENTY-SEVEN YEARS I NEVER MISSED A DAY'S WORK because of drinking. However hung-over I might be, with however little sleep, I forced myself to go to work, even if it meant taking three drinks before breakfast to rally my determination.

This isn't a testimonial for drinking—or for a curious form of will power, either. I mention the point just to show that a person can be an alcoholic and still *appear* to be doing his job. I knew a managing editor, a great newspaperman for years, who lived that way. If he drank until five A.M., he got up at seven, cursing, shouting, giving commands, determined to be more vigorous than anyone who might have had two drinks and gone to bed at midnight. In his later years he still cursed and shouted—but his commands made little sense.

All of this came back to me this morning when we held a special program of our own—patients only, no staff—in our dorm. Men and women told how they drank, what they drank, and why they wanted to stop. Spree drinkers, unlike me and the managing editor, described how they would go for weeks, perhaps months, without drinking—then stay drunk for weeks, perhaps months.

Our program had no rigid structure; patients could speak of whatever they wished. Mrs. Gibson, a grandmother who works in a tobacco plant, said often she would drink almost anything she could lay her hands on. "One night in the dark," she said, "I meant to get the vanilla extract but I got some cake coloring. I woke up in the morning with green all over me and I thought I had caught something terrible."

A few other patients said they had drunk paint thinner and shaving lotion. But the majority said they stuck to accepted alcoholic beverages, or at least moonshine. Two younger men said they sometimes took amphetamines and drank at the same time. But Tip Watson said, "Those pills will kill you. I don't fool with pills."

Ralph Leonard is a pleasant man to be around, and he speaks well. He told of his experiences. "I thought I was a better mathematician drunk than most were sober. I believed that for a long while, but something strange started happening. My figures weren't coming out right. I enjoyed drinking. I enjoyed going to new places and meeting interesting people. Then I found I was meeting all sorts of interesting people—interesting cops, interesting sheriffs, interesting highway patrolmen, interesting lawyers, interesting bondsmen, interesting judges. I finally decided I had met enough interesting people."

The program went on for about an hour, some of it fairly searching. Then Mr. Harper, who has an artificial right leg, said well, it might not seem like much of a reason to quit drinking, but he had one: "This last time when I had to go to the hospital I was so drunk I didn't know where I was, but I could walk. I went through the main lobby in nothing but my drawers and my wooden leg. I don't want to do that again."

Men quit for different reasons, and one is as good as another.

Bill Carroll, who is in charge of vocational rehabilitation services here, is a good lecturer. His material is to the point and he gets his audience involved. It's a disparate audience, too—made up of men and women from all three dorms and men from D Dorm at the Big Top.

"Let's say you were hiring a man," Carroll said, standing beside a blackboard. "What qualities would you look for?"

"Ability," someone said. "Good appearance," someone else said.

"Sure," Carroll said. "Let's write them down." He started writing on the board. "We'll say it's 1951 when we hire this person." He wrote 1951 over the top of the column. "What else?"

"Be on time."

"Honest."

"Intelligence."

"Loyal."

"Dependable."

"Good manners."

"Be stable."

"Good health."

"Good personality."

"Right," Carroll said. "That's an important one— being able to get along with people. Any more?" He started writing again. "Over here, we'll put 1971— twenty years later—and we'll make two columns. Assets and Liabilities." He drew the columns and labeled them. "Let's say that when we hired the man he drank a little—a beer after work or a couple drinks on the weekend. Okay? But about here [he was following a horizontal line from 1951 to 1971], he starts drinking more. About here, he's missing work some. Here, his employer speaks to him. And now he's drinking steadily, having trouble with memory. He's missing work more, too. His employer thinks he will have to fire him. He can't stop drinking. It's 1971 now. Let's look at the qualities we put down in 1951. Does the man still have them all? We'll move them over here to 1971 and list them under assets or liabilities. All right?"

He began calling out the qualities, letting us decide

in which column they should be listed. Most of them were placed quickly, provoking no discussion. Only on intelligence was there disagreement.

"You don't ever lose that," a man said, "if you had any in the first place." He was a new man in A Dorm, big, with a thick neck, and he said he was a building contractor. "I take about six drinks and I can really read a set of blueprints."

"Shit," somebody said.

"I'm telling you a man never loses intelligence," the contractor said.

"The hell he doesn't."

"Well, it depends," someone else said, "on what you mean by intelligence."

"Let's put it down as an asset," Bill Carroll said, the only time he entered the discussion. "In 1971 the man still has it."

When we finished listing, intelligence was the only quality under "Assets." The others had become "Liabilities." There it was in writing, dictated by alcoholics: the man with eleven good qualities had one left—and it was in doubt.

As we left the lecture, one of the men in our dorm said, "You know that big contractor? Night before last, when he'd just got here, he was behind me in the cafeteria. I had to show him how to get his milk out of the machine."

It's not hard to study a hypothetical man, examining what happened to him in twenty years. You can write off with little pain his good qualities. You're being honest with him, right? But when you examine your own twenty years, it is with less certainty. I'm not sure how much I lost, but I want it back. And I want more—qualities that I *never* had. Each day I spend here, I feel better about my chances.

Tuesday

>◁<

Not all of our group therapy sessions explode
with sudden insights and wisdom, the way they do on
television. But there is a cumulative effect, a good
one, as we discuss our lives and listen to other alcoholics discuss theirs.

Certainly in my own case, it has been helpful to be
around men like Mr. Wellington and Coley Thompson. I see clearly the similarities in our behavior, even
if their unassertiveness is far more pronounced than
my own. At first I was reluctant to admit that—even
to myself. And surely it was not to my taste to sit in
a room and tell six other persons that I was, in some
ways, a lot like pitiful, gentle, broken Mr. Wellington.
Or like Coley Thompson, nervous, his stomach gone,
his words falling over each other as he offers you candy
or chewing gum.

It is necessary, however, for an alcoholic to meet his failings squarely. (If that sounds like an old drunk's Boy Scout motto, at least it makes sense to old drunks.) So this morning, in answer to a question by Weldon Bayliss, I tried to explain why I drank. However it came out, it was a start: "I don't know exactly. I wasn't happy a lot of the time. I guess whiskey gave me some kind of peace. Maybe it's what we've been talking about—standing up for our rights. The way you told Mr. Wellington he's been letting people push him around. And Coley . . . what he's said about how he lived. I guess I've been the same way."

"Well, what are you going to do about it?" Bayliss asked.

"I've been thinking about it," I said. "When I get out of here I don't want to be a mean son of a bitch all the time, but I'm going to try to tell people when something bothers me."

"That's it," Bayliss said. "Often it's just small things, but you shouldn't let them pass, because if you do they will eat at you later. You don't have to be *mean*—just stand up for your rights. I had a woman take up three parking spaces in Chapel Hill this morning. Just went in on an angle and took them all. Now, I could have circled around, looking for another place, but if I had, it would have bothered me later. I would have said to myself, 'Doggone it, Bayliss, why didn't you *do* something?' But I got out of the car and said, 'Could you straighten up a little so I would have room to get in?' That's all there was to it."

He turned to Mr. Wade, a retired sanitation worker. "Why do you drink, Mr. Wade?"

"When people are coming over to the house, I get nervous. Relatives or friends, you know. I have a hard time talking to them unless I drink some."

"You don't feel comfortable, then, in social situations?"

"No, sir," Mr. Wade said. He seemed to be thinking. "And when I get ready to do a chore. I don't know why, but I'd take a drink before I went out to cut my grass or work in my garden. Then I got to coming in out of my garden to get another drink."

No one offered any theories about that.

"Why do you drink, Mr. Thompson?" Bayliss asked. "Have you figured out really *why*?"

"It's like I said before," Coley replied, "I don't have anything to do. I just sit in the house all day. I do cook a lot. I like to cook. Nell comes home from work and I have a big stew sitting on the stove. Nell is crazy about how I fix stew." Coley said he doesn't drink at all on days his young grandchildren are alone with him, visiting. "If something happened to those children, like the house caught fire, I'd kill myself."

Mr. Wellington said that he was concerned about his wife. "She was in the hospital for more than a month and I hope she'll be all right. She . . . she was very sick. She was sick like this once before, about four years ago." Mr. Wellington paused. "We thought she'd be better."

Our time was running out. "I hope your wife will be all right," Bayliss said. "I know it makes your life difficult."

I stayed after the group session to ask Bayliss if I could go camping next weekend. On a patient's third weekend at ARC, he can go wherever he chooses if he has his counselor's permission. I suppose that's to give him a taste of outside life before he leaves ARC permanently. I told Bayliss that I wanted to camp in a state park near Danbury, North Carolina. It would be the long Memorial Day weekend.

"Fine," he said.

I then asked him if I could leave ARC before completing my full twenty-eight days. Many patients do that. Some counselors seem even to advocate it, feeling that when a patient "peaks" in his understanding he shouldn't be kept around for repetition. I explained that the owner of a chain of newspapers had scheduled meetings with his editors and publishers and wanted me to talk to them. That would mean leaving ARC four days early.

"Let's talk about it in a few days," Bayliss said. "I think you're getting along well."

Giving up whiskey, I believe, may be easier than giving up cigarettes. When I quit smoking three years ago, I went for weeks, months, constantly wanting a cigarette. But not drinking during the time I've been here hasn't bothered me. There was just the fishing trip, when I could "taste" a drink and a cigarette. I haven't wanted a drink since but I've wanted a cigarette.

I went this afternoon, as I do many afternoons, to talk with Nancy Laidlaw. I wanted to ask her about the fishing trip and my cravings. She was seated at her desk in an orange miniskirt that I had not seen before, looking as she always does: as if she were about to discover something but wouldn't get too excited about it when she did. That's one of the reasons I like her—she doesn't swarm on you with psychological zeal. Or any other kind. She's in her late twenties, tall, with dark hair to her shoulders, a western North Carolina mountain girl who added an interesting layer of something—sophistication? not quite—during the three years that she lived in New York's East Village.

"Why did it come on me so strong during the fishing trip?" I asked her.

"Maybe it's associations," she said. "Good times you had on other fishing trips, smoking and drinking."

"Maybe. But I was never a big fisherman, in the first place. I would just get a rowboat and take my son out in Cold Spring Harbor, sitting in the sunshine, having a good time being with him."

"Drinking?"

"Sometimes I'd take a six-pack of beer."

"Smoking?"

"Not for three years, and we fished a lot after that. Had a good time."

"I don't know," Nancy said. "What do *you* think?"

"I don't know, either. I don't have the slightest urge now to drink, but I certainly want to smoke."

"It's tough," Nancy said. "I'm trying to quit myself. Maybe it's the old oral need."

I left pondering the problem, almost sure that I would start smoking soon.

On the way to the cafeteria, I met Tip Watson and

we had dinner together. With a lot of twilight left, Tip and I circled the quadrangle, enabling him to make his rounds, complete his evening check of patients.

Tip paused beside a bench. "Let's go across the river, Mr. Leland," he said, "and *get* one."

We walked on.

"Hello, Pilot. Little faster, Mr. Wellington."

And to Luther Moore, the quiet man who works in a factory: "You out here bothering people, Luther, with all your fuss? I'll call a 'tenant [attendant] to you."

We met Johnny Ross, who is still upset about not being able to go home.

"Durocher won't let me," Johnny said. "It's on my papers."

As we moved on, Tip said, "Johnny ain't telling it all. If he signed in here on his own, like he claims, he could go any time he pleased. Somebody committed that boy. Maybe his momma or his wife."

I left Tip at A Dorm, where there is a cigarette machine. I studied all of the brands, looking at each several times, and passed over the one that I had liked three years ago. I selected a brand that I had heard didn't taste good but was supposed to be "safer." I walked back to the dorm, smoking, not feeling good about it, and got a quart can of grapefruit juice from the refrigerator. Tonight, writing, I smoked most of the cigarettes and drank all of the juice. I felt bad about smoking but I was glad I had drunk a quart of juice, not a quart of vodka.

Wednesday

✕

OUR NAMES CHECKED OFF PROPERLY, WE LOADED ON
the blue bus for the drive to recreation. We were
about to start when Tip Watson called out, "Mr. Leland, you back there?" There was no answer. "Well,
sir," Tip said, "he's finally done it. Mr. Leland has
gone across the river to *get* one."

Charley, studying his list, said, "Leland's not
Monday-Wednesday. He's Tuesday-Thursday."

"Do you suppose," Tip said to me, "that Charley
figures a man would run off without a stitch of clothes
except what he's got on, when he could pack a bag
any time and strike out through the woods?"

"Charley hasn't got time for figuring," I said. "He
lost a prisoner the other day." He had, as a matter of
fact; at least someone had. For an hour or so a man
was unaccounted for when he had been sent over to

Umstead for X-rays without the proper persons being told.

"Charley," I said, "I understand you're not a hundred percent any more. You lost one."

"That's not true," Charley said. "I didn't lose him. The rec people lost him."

"They told me *you* lost him."

"Well, that's not so," Charley said. "*They* lost him."

He gave the back of the bus a couple good looks, kept his eye on the rear-view mirror, and we were on our way.

I've been sidetracked a while on my woodcut. Pat Carroll's child was sick, and she couldn't work with us. Then Pat herself was sick. During that time I suffered a lack of guidance. Well, Tip came in sometimes from shooting basketball to offer counsel, and Julie Ryan, whose mushrooms look quite good, actually did help me. Pat had headed me on my way toward drawing the picture, but when it came to *cutting* it, and Pat wasn't there, I had trouble. I wasn't sure which portions to chisel out, so they would not print, and which portions to leave unchiseled, so they would print. I got impatient with the big sections, the sky and ocean, and gouged at them with the biggest chisel I could find. One day I went out in the sunshine and shot "21" with Tip; he beat me. Another day we took the golf clubs out front, where there is three hundred yards of unbroken grass, but we didn't need that much for our drives. Tip strides at the ball, as if he were taking a baseball swing, and except for one ball that he caught just right and popped into the woods, the three hundred yards contained us both.

Today Julie and a young man who works in the recreation program offered to help me print the woodcut. I had declared it completed. Double-printing it, first red and then blue, a few times reversing the second impression, we got a . . . well, what we got was a work that reflects an immense primitive strength and at the same time a sophisticated sense of impressionism, making a statement on Contemporary Society.

Walking to group therapy, Tip and I talked with Mr. Wade about his garden, how he drank while he worked on it.

"You sure you telling Bailey the whole thing?" Tip asked. He appeared serious. He studied Mr. Wade.

"It was just like I told him," Mr. Wade said. "I used to take a drink before I went out there, then I got to coming back to the house to get another one. Same with cutting the grass."

"That's not exactly how I heard it," Tip said. "I heard you used to take a drink for the whole garden, got to taking a drink a row, and finally got to a drink for ever plant. Now ain't that the shape of it, Mr. Wade?"

Mr. Wade smiled.

"Bill and me can save you a lot of trouble," Tip said. "We'll come up there and pave that whole damn garden. Your front yard, too."

If there is a single tenet at ARC that dominates all others, it is that an alcoholic can never drink again, not any amount, as long as he lives. That point is made in films, lectures, group therapy, literature, AA meetings, and conversations among patients.

Despite all that, there was this question and reply at our group session today:

Bayliss: "Mr. Moore, how will you get along when you go home?"

Luther Moore: "All right. I'm not going to drink as much."

A friendship, almost a tenderness, has developed in our group, and Julie Ryan said, "Luther, we can't drink *anything*. None of us."

Luther was silent, and I tried to make him feel better. "When you've been drinking as long as we have, it's a strange feeling, isn't it—to think you can't ever have another drop. You remember that doctor in the film who said, 'Not even a glass of sherry at Christmas.'"

Again Luther made no reply. I wondered if he understood the point yet—that he could never drink anything again.

Sitting in my room tonight, thinking about Luther, I realized that he has an added strike against him. I don't think I'll ever have trouble again with whiskey, but if I do, it won't be because I don't understand the problem and some of the solutions.

Thursday

⋈

THE MAGNIFICENT DR. D STRODE IN THIS MORNING, carrying his liver in a sack. Two livers. A "hobnail" liver and a perfectly good one.

"Here comes Durocher with his damn liver," a D Dorm man said.

Heads turned, and we watched Dr. Desrosiers and his sack move to the front of the auditorium. He did not require us to inspect the hobnail liver, as old-timers had said flatly that he would—"*makes* you look at it." Rather, he placed the two livers, neatly wrapped in transparent coverings, on the lectern and invited us to come forward after his lecture and compare the bad liver and the good liver, if we chose.

Turning to a blackboard, on which he sketched throughout his talk, Dr. Desrosiers said, "I am speaking this morning on the liver." He looked about the

98

room, spotting faces of "repeaters." "Some of you have heard this lecture, but it won't do you any harm to hear it again." He pointed out that he was not here to scare us, as some might suspect, but to discuss simply the ability, and the inability, of the liver to handle alcohol.

His sentences were precise and his tone quiet; he is a fine lecturer. Unlike the afternoon when he and I talked for two hours, he held himself in a bit this morning, not looping through a half-dozen layers of classical thought. He stuck to the liver. Although his talk was less lofty, I would guess that his performances are always much the same, whether for one person or a thousand: he enjoys putting his mind out there where he can see it, and you can, too.

If there is any alcohol to be found normally in the human body, he explained, it is an infinitesimal amount. The liver's ability to deal with that is far more than adequate. But putting great quantities of alcohol into the body by drinking is another matter.

"In the average-sized male," Dr. Desrosiers said, "the liver can detoxify three-quarters of an ounce of ethyl alcohol per hour, or about seven to eight small drops of the substance per minute. Now, is there anyone here who uses alcohol in those small amounts?"

On the board, he sketched the liver's desperate struggle to deal with large amounts of alcohol, showing how it became damaged and attempted to repair itself by producing new cells to replace ones that had been destroyed. It was not a good-looking liver that he drew. After his lecture, some went forward to inspect the two livers, the hobnail one (which he said got its name from the boot) looking bumpy, the other looking smooth. Some others did not go for the inspection. I did, and although I know very little about livers, I hoped fervently that mine looked like the good one. When I had my physical examination the first day here, the young doctor indicated that I was in good shape. Having drunk enough to hurt myself seriously, I felt fortunate. That feeling comes often now, and it increases my determination not to drink. It's almost religious, I suppose, a feeling that I have been given an unimpaired second chance.

When a patient leaves Butner, should his old friends, family members, and business associates hide their bottles? Not drink around him?

That question arose during our group therapy session today, and I thought the answer was obvious— no, it wouldn't make sense. He could be around people who drink. But I was the only one in the group who seemed to hold that view. Well, Julie Ryan might agree, at least in theory.

Like many subjects that we discuss, this one came up obliquely. Julie was reflecting on the problems that she and her husband, Skip, have in their marriage: "Sometimes he just takes off by himself for the beach, or somewhere, without even bothering to ask if I would like to go. Just a couple weeks after the baby was born, I had to go accept a civic award for him. He was off at the beach. I wanted to throw the damn thing in his face." She looked forward, she said, to discussing these things with him at a husband-wife seminar to be held here this weekend. "I really do," she said. "I'm going to tell him a lot of things. I resent his drinking—and I'm going to say so."

"He shouldn't drink around you," Coley Thompson said. "Not when he knows you got the problem."

"That's right," Mr. Wade said. "There shouldn't be any whiskey in the house."

"Suppose a friend comes over?" I asked.

"If you want to quit drinking," Coley said, "you can't be around a bunch of people who do."

"Hell, I'd have to get out of the newspaper business," I said. "Everybody drinks. Are you going to join a monastery, or what?"

"Well, what I really resent," Julie said, "is Skip pretending in public that he doesn't drink around me—then coming home and drinking. It's the hypocrisy that burns me."

"I still think you got to keep away from people who drink," Coley said.

"I do, too," Jack Harris, a cabdriver, said.

We debated the point at some length, my position being that I could make the decision not to drink, but I didn't have any business imposing it on anyone else. In the first place, I said, it would be impossible; in the second place, I didn't want to. "I'm not going to quit going around with friends I've liked all my life. And if they want a drink, they ought to be able to have one."

I didn't mean to sound superior, or good-sportish,

either; I was just trying to make a point that I believe: if a person is going to stop drinking, he has to be able to do it regardless of what anyone else does.

Well, the idea will be tested soon enough because I certainly have a lot of friends who drink.

Friday

⋈

Sometime before daylight, it started raining hard, and it's still raining. I have kept up with the weather forecasts, even called the weather bureau in Raleigh, and I hope that it will be dry when I camp tomorrow night. The forecast is for clearing, but either way, wet or dry, I am going.

After breakfast this morning, I went to the administration building to get a form that I will use tomorrow to get my car for the weekend. It has been parked in a lot across the street from the police station, with police holding the keys. (This is done with all patients who bring cars; few do.) The form, filled out by the woman who annoyed me the first day I came here by calling me "Bill," will authorize the police to give me my car. Today, as we talked, the woman said, "Bill, I'm happy that you're getting along so well." I thanked her, calling her "Phyllis," which I had always refused to do. She's okay. When you've been off whiskey a while, and you're not frightened or angry, you see people differently.

Several patients left this afternoon for the long weekend. Tip Watson's boss drove over and picked him up. Tip will spend the holiday working at his old job. Paul Evans went home to talk with his wife, to decide whether they might go back together after being separated for four years. I'll drop Mr. Wellington off at his home tomorrow on my way to Hanging Rock State Park.

Before our group therapy session this morning, I asked Weldon Bayliss what he had decided about my leaving Butner next Thursday. "I don't see why not," he said, "if everything goes well for you this weekend."

Much of the session was taken up with that—our thoughts of how the weekend would be. If anyone had fears or reservations, he didn't express them directly. Bayliss started with Mr. Wellington: "Do you see any problems, Mr. Wellington?"

"Well, no. No, sir . . . I hope my wife is better. I hope she will be all right."

"Mr. Evans?" Bayliss asked.

"I think my wife and I can talk now," Paul said. "We really will try to decide what to do. My girls need me at home with them."

"Mr. McIlwain?"

"I'll be fine. I hope it stops raining."

"Mr. Watson?"

"Fine," Tip said. "I'm going to work at my old job."

"The whole weekend?"

"Yes, sir."

That's all Tip said, but I had an uneasy feeling. Not that he would get drunk this weekend, but that he won't come back. Julie Ryan told me she had said to him, kidding, "Come back sober," and Tip replied, "If you think I can't come back sober, maybe I won't come back."

Tip is much more sensitive, I believe, than most people realize. I also believe that his life outside is a hard one on which to stay sober. One afternoon, in hot sunshine, we took off our shirts and sat in the grass behind the dorm, talking. "You know what my brother used to say to me? 'Well, you been sober two weeks, you'll probably be drunk tomorrow'—and sometimes I was." Tip said that when he wasn't drinking, his friends would say, "What's the matter— you not man enough to take a drink?" I thought how different my friends would be. All of them. The last thing they would ever do would be try to push me into taking a drink.

That afternoon behind the dorm, Tip and I talked for two hours. We ranged over many things, and he told me about d.t.'s. "You don't just see snakes and spiders, like you hear about," he said. "You see people . . . sometimes real people you know . . . as real as you are right now. One time a boy who had been dead two weeks, a good friend of mine, came in the room, and I said, 'Tommy, leave me alone. Just go away.' He kept coming at me and I got out of bed and swung at him. Another time I saw three men out in my yard getting ready to hang two boys, friends of mine, and the looked up in the window and saw me and said, 'We'll get that son of a bitch next.' I called the sheriff's office and said they was about to be a hanging in my yard, three fellows hanging two friends of mine, and pretty soon here comes that blue light and the siren, two deputies. But my brother sent them away." Tip smiled at that, but said, "It's all just as real as you sitting there right now."

Tip jokes a lot, giving the appearance of not being serious, but he is. "I hope you make it," he said. "Lee looks like a good girl. I liked her." He paused, seeming wistful, I thought. "I had it worked out pretty good once," he said, "but I messed it up. I had a job at a big estate, was the gardener, and I liked it. Stayed out in the sun all day, working, by myself. I had a real nice girl and we were living in an apartment, getting along fine, and I hadn't had a drink for nine months. One afternoon after work, it was real hot and I thought I could have one beer. I drank it and was going out the door when a friend of mine came up and said have one with him. He said he wanted to show me his new car, and we took it out on the Interstate for a ride. 'Let's get a pint and have a couple of gin bucks,' he said. 'Just a couple.' We got the gin and it was seven days before I went home."

Tip, rolling a piece of grass between his fingers, looked up at me. "Work hard at it," he said. "Lee likes you. You're smart and you can get a good job. You got a lot to lose."

"Tip, you've got as much to lose as I have. I believe

wherever you've been, you've helped somebody. Working at all your jobs. People had to be happier because you were around them."

He didn't reply to that; still looking at me, he just said again, "I hope you make it."

There was a wistfulness, a sadness, about him, this kind, funny man, that moved me more than anything has since I have been at Butner. As plainly as if he had spoken the words, he was telling me, I thought, that he didn't have a chance, but I did.

Saturday

✠

I T WAS STILL RAINING THIS MORNING, HARD, AND A
young attendant drove me to the police station to pick
up my car. Four policemen sat in chairs around the
tiny room and another was at the desk. I approached
him, handed him the form, and told him what I
wanted. Behind me, I heard one of the men say something, but I didn't understand what he said and I
didn't realize he was speaking to me. He spoke again:
"Good day for drinking, ain't it, Preacher?" I knew
then he was speaking to me, but I didn't turn.

A policeman on my left said, "He's talking to you."
I turned.

"It's a good day for drinking, ain't it, Preacher?"
the cop said.

"Do you think that's funny?" I asked him.

"I don't think it's funny," he said. He was a man
about my size, a little younger.

108

"Then mind your own business."

"I didn't say it was funny."

"If you ever had the problem," I said, "you wouldn't think it was funny."

"*You* think it's funny?" he said.

"Don't say anything else to me," I said. I felt my head and chest thumping. "Don't say anything."

No one spoke as the officer at the desk gave me the keys and I walked out into the rain. A police car followed me while I drove the few blocks on Central Avenue, before turning toward ARC, but he may not have been trying to trap me.

At the dorm, there were only seven people, including the "Pilot" and Mr. Wellington, who had been sitting in the lobby with his shaving kit since breakfast, waiting to ride with me to his home. I asked them if they would sit down and talk, that I wanted to tell them what had happened. I was still upset. I had thought the cops would lead me into hitting the man, and I hadn't wanted to. He must sit there taking cheap, ignorant shots at every ARC patient who comes to pick up his car. Talking to the patients, I felt better. Bobby Felt, the bus driver, said, "The dirty bastard . . . but it's a good thing you didn't hit him."

"Let's go home, Mr. Wellington," I said. "Let's get on the big road." He smiled.

The rental business where Tip Watson works is on our way, and I had told Tip I would stop by. He was working behind the building, helping two other men load chairs into a truck. "Hello, Mr. Wellington," he said, "you getting ready to go home and have yourself a time?"

Mr. Wellington nodded.

I told Tip we would be coming back Monday afternoon and I would take him to Butner.

"I don't know," Tip said. "I may not go back."

I hoped he would, I said. Bayliss was going to let me leave Thursday, I told him, and he probably would let Tip go, too. We could all ride together—Mr. Wellington, Tip, and I.

"I appreciate that," Tip said.

"We'll pick you up Monday," I said.

"If I'm going," Tip said, "I'll have all my stuff here."

As we rode on Interstate 85, Mr. Wellington said, "Do you think he'll go back?"

"I don't know," I said.

Mr. Wellington lives in a red brick house in the center of town, and when I turned around in his driveway I saw a garden in his backyard. "Somebody's been taking care of your garden, Mr. Wellington. It looks good."

"It does," he said. "We'll have some nice tomatoes."

It was dark—and still raining—when I got to Hanging Rock, just before the chain was to be locked across the entrance to the park for the night. Everything was wet and I couldn't get a fire started. Facing the car around, I worked by headlights, stumbling over roots, having a hell of a time getting the tent up, but I went to sleep feeling good.

Sunday

><

I HAVE CAMPED A GREAT DEAL, OFTEN IN BAD WEATH-
er, and always with a fifth of bourbon.

Once on an island in Lake George, New York, I
watched a great windstorm, carrying sheets of rain, roll
across the lake and rip my campsite. Beside the Yad-
kin River in North Carolina, I slept little through a
night of sleet and ice. On Fire Island, New York, in
blistering sun, without a leaf of shade, I struggled for
an hour with an umbrella tent, trying, as it turned out,
to put it up backwards.

Through rain, sleet, wind, and sun, I drank.

Just at daybreak this morning, as I stood among the
wet, cold oaks and pines at Hanging Rock State Park,
near Danbury, North Carolina, I concluded two
things: (1) adversity has a map of the state and na-
tional parks and knows my schedule; (2) I had no
desire to drink.

I had been dry during the night, but cold. The tent was on a slope, and several times in my sleep I had edged downhill, leaving both blankets behind. Wanting to make coffee and breakfast, I searched without success for dry wood. The rain had turned to drizzle, but it made no difference. For three days water had soaked the ground, and globules hung in trees above. Poking around a fireplace, I found half-dry wood in the remains of an old fire. Using newspaper and all of the lighter fluid that I had, a pint, I could not get a fire going. I got in the car, to go to Danbury to get more lighter fluid. But fifty yards from my tent, I found a shelter—I had not seen it in the night—filled with dry wood, operating on the honor system. A bundle of wood for twenty-five cents. I made a fire, fanning it with a baking pan, and had breakfast.

After breakfast I walked a long way, in and out of drizzle, down a trail that led first to a stream, then a lake. It is beautiful country, even in bad weather, and I decided that I would return sometime.

In early afternoon it had stopped raining and I rode to Danbury, a small town, and found a country store, one of the few places open on Sunday. I bought two cans of Vienna sausages, a box of saltine crackers, a Pepsi, and the *Winston-Salem Journal-Sentinel*. Taking them to a wall beside the old brick courthouse in the center of town, I sat for an hour, reading, eating, and thinking. Thinking at first about having just seen a farmer buy a six-pack of beer in the country store. Many towns and cities in North Carolina don't sell beer on Sunday, but Danbury does. There had been nothing unusual about the purchase—a man taking a six-pack from the refrigerator and paying the proprietor—but it set my thoughts ranging. How many six-packs I had bought in so many towns.

Sitting there in the quiet afternoon, it was as if my life were doubling back on me, letting me see more clearly what it had been and what it might become. I had worked on this newspaper, the one I was reading now, twenty years ago, and in this same country town I had persuaded a deputy sheriff to let me inside a jail cell to talk with a man who had killed his wife and her lover. In an hour he would be let out to attend her funeral, and then brought back. Waiting, he talked with me, explaining why he had killed them both. "He was working my molds," he said. "The whole time I was in prison, he was working my molds. When I came home and found out, I had to kill them both." His molds were ones with which he made the plaster figures of animals that you see in front yards along rural roads. He gave me a small white cat with red ears—I don't know why he had it with him in jail—and the cat has traveled with me from North Carolina, to Virginia, to New York, and back. That was the last story I ever wrote for that newspaper—and the best, I think—and I did it knowing it was good. It was a time when I still felt easy and saw no trouble ahead; before Virginia and New York, when I became afraid. I will not get back exactly that ease, the kind that existed when I thought that nothing could ever go wrong—but it would be foolish to want it. The dangers in my life, behind and in front, seem clear. What

Butner has done is help me believe I can see danger and fend it off.

Driving the six miles back to my campsite, I thought specifically of the incident in the police station yesterday. Surely in the past I would not have acted as I did. It was no great moment of courage, but I had done what I was supposed to do: I had told the cop I didn't like what he was saying to me. Before Butner and Weldon Bayliss ("Fight 'em at the flagpole, Mr. Wellington"), I may have said nothing or, worse, said something amiable and smiled. And just as surely, too, I would have felt bad all day and maybe the next day —cursing the cop to myself, believing I was still bothered by him but bothered actually, as Bayliss says, by myself—by my failure to stand up for my rights.

I made a fire, cooked a steak, and sat on a stump, smoking and drinking coffee, thinking about myself and the people I have met at Butner. I would pick up Mr. Wellington tomorrow and I hoped I would pick up Tip Watson, too.

Monday

>⟡<

As I OPENED THE CAR DOOR AFTER PULLING INTO MR. Wellington's driveway, he appeared on the steps, carrying his shaving kit and a small bag. He had been waiting.

"How're you, Mr. Wellington?"

"Fine . . . I'm fine."

"Have a good weekend?"

"Yes. Well . . . yes." Mr. Wellington always sounds tentative, often breaking his thoughts with pauses. "Yours all right?"

"It was wet," I said, "but I enjoyed it. Hanging Rock is a pretty park."

We weren't a half-mile from his home when he said, "I drank some beer."

I didn't say anything.

"Just a couple," he said. "Three."

The first thing I felt was "What the hell's wrong with you, Mr. Wellington? Are you crazy?" But all I said was "When?"

"Saturday," he said. "Saturday night. Just three."

I honestly didn't know what to say. It surprised me more than anything that has happened since I've been at Butner. All the obvious reactions came to me: He's been told a hundred times that he can't ever drink *anything* . . . but he comes home for just a weekend and drinks.

"I got a little tense," he said. "You know . . . at home. I drank it after supper."

I had the feeling that he had been waiting all day, almost two days, to tell me—and he had: "I told my wife I was going to tell Bill as soon as he came."

What the hell was I supposed to do about it?

"My wife wasn't well as . . . I hoped she would be."

"I hope you'll tell Bayliss," I said. "Or Dr. Desrosiers."

"I don't want to stay any extra time. If I tell them, they might hold me over."

Throughout our entire conversation, I had to hold back my thoughts: *Good God, what are you at Butner for? You come home on a visit and drink and don't want to tell anybody. What's going to happen when you come home for good?*

"I just had the three," he said. "I didn't drink any yesterday."

He wanted me to tell him it was all right.

"You should talk with Bayliss," I said. "Or somebody down there."

"I don't want to stay any extra time."

"I understand that," I said. "But even if you had to stay a little longer . . . You don't want to drink when you come home."

"I'm going to take the . . ."

"Antabuse?"

"Yes. I'm going to take that."

"Then you really should talk to them. They may not think you should take it."

"I believe it would help me with my job. It might help get me back."

We were on the Interstate now and Mr. Wellington was repeating himself: "I just drank those three."

"Well, you know . . . they said we can't drink anything at all."

"I took a little ammonia yesterday morning," Mr. Wellington said. "Just a little, mixed with Pepsi. For my nerves."

"I would talk to them," I said. "Tell Dr. Desrosiers. He's a good man."

"My niece brought the children over and they messed up the house. I had to fix it. I didn't want my wife to get upset." He hesitated. "My niece does it all the time . . . brings the children over and they mess up the house. So she can go around town."

"Did you tell her? Ask her not to do that?"

"No. No . . . I didn't tell her. She's got a hot temper."

"Well, you've got to tell her." I was getting sick of the conversation, starting to feel as if I thought I was a counselor. And I was getting annoyed with Mr. Wellington, a gentle, pitiful man.

"Do you think they would make me stay extra time?"

"I don't know. I don't have any idea. Ask them."

"My wife wasn't as well as I hoped she would be."

"I'm sorry," I said.

"Do you think Tip will go back with us?" Mr. Wellington asked.

"I don't know."

We were almost at Tip's exit and we rode in silence.

I knew when I saw Tip that he wasn't going. He was standing outside the building, unloading a truck.

"Have a good weekend, Mr. Wellington?" Tip asked. "You stay sober?"

"Well, I . . . yes, had a good weekend." It seemed for a moment that he might be about to tell Tip about the beer. But Tip interrupted him: "Good. You didn't have to whip anybody?"

"Will you ride back with us, Tip?" I asked.

"No, I guess not," he said. "I'll just stay here on the job. But I appreciate it. Will you call me?"

"Sure."

"I mean it."

"Yes, I will."

"I wouldn't drink if I thought you were going to call me. Ask Julie to call me, too."

"All right."

"You can tell Bailey I decided to stay home."

"Okay."

We shook hands, and I said, "Take good care, Tip."

"I will," he said. "You, too." He looked at me and smiled. "I want you to make it."

As we got back on the road and rode toward Butner, I felt that two of our group had already been shot down.

Tuesday

><

As the time approaches for me to leave Butner, I have thought a great deal about what the ARC program can do—and cannot do—for an alcoholic.

One thing it can't do is work blinding magic. If a person comes here solely because of someone else's insistence—say, the threats or pleas of a wife or boss—he's wasting his time. And everybody else's. Dr. Desrosiers may compose music and build airplanes, but he waves no wand that sends a man home dry and happy—with a lifetime guarantee. As Desrosiers himself says, an alcoholic first must have strong motivation; then perhaps the ARC can show him how to succeed.

In my own twenty-two days here, many things have been of help—lectures, films, group therapy sessions, conversations, and experiences. But none of it, singly, stands out in my mind as having brought deep, new insight. Much of what I have heard and seen, I had heard and seen before. So why has the place been good for me? Surely one of the reasons has to be that Butner has given me a period of quiet time—spent in a different setting—to sort out, test, and pull together some of my thinking. I came here wanting very much to quit drinking—but not at all convinced that I could function well or enjoy myself without whiskey. The days here have offered considerable evidence that I can. Some of the evidence might seem curiously slight, or unimportant, but I needed it.

Fooling around with Tip Watson, for instance, I found that I still liked to joke and laugh. I hadn't been sure that whimsy occurred to a sober man. When the patients elected me dorm leader, it gave me a feeling of worth—to myself and to them. It struck me, of course, as ironic that I once had led mighty forces and devised mighty plans, but hadn't felt especially worthwhile.

Talking with Dr. Desrosiers, a man whose references range across a half-dozen levels of classic thought, I hadn't been uneasy, even at times when I didn't know what the hell he was talking about. I have, in the past, felt uneasy in the presence of fools.

Being around Nancy Laidlaw, maybe just because of her nature, I found that psychiatry and psychology could be casual and pragmatic—not just about toilet training, phallic symbols, and ids. Talking one day about whether I should take Antabuse (a drug that will make you violently ill if you drink), she said,

"If you feel you don't need it, don't take it. But if you start worrying about drinking on an impulse, start taking Antabuse." Another time about depression: "If it hits you, don't sit there and try to analyze it on the spot, wondering what caused it. Whatever you're doing at the time, stop if it's at all possible and do something else. That helps get you out of depression, then you can try to figure it out later."

Lee's visit, and her seeming to enjoy me, made me realize a man didn't have to be turned-on all the time, charming the leaves right off bushes. I had lived that way a long while, wound up, defoliating everything in sight.

Weldon Bayliss, the big-boned preacher in drip-dry shirts and narrow neckties, made me know all over again that content is more important than style. He may fall all over himself in his earnestness, an unlikely-looking man to be consorting with drunks—but he believes what he's saying, and pretty soon I did, too.

And I found—maybe the most important thing of all—that giving up whiskey apparently was not going to be an hour-after-hour, day-after-day struggle for me, gnawed all the while by wanting a drink but having to fight it off. I haven't felt that at all here. If I had, I don't think I would make it. The endlessness of it, the prospect of hanging on forever by sheer will, would be too much. That's probably why so many "recovered" alcoholics kill themselves: they've made the decision never to drink again, and stick by it, but can't stand the terrible effort.

A Farewell to Alcohol

The question of whether or not to take Antabuse is an interesting one. With just a half-tablet a day, a person can guarantee himself of one certainty: if he so much as tastes alcohol, he will become sick. A D Dorm man described it to me: "I never been so sick in my life. They put me in an ambulance and took me to the hospital and pumped my stomach. I thought for sure I was dying."

But if a man wants to drink, all he has to do is stop taking the tablets, allow five to ten days for the Antabuse to clear his system, and start drinking. Even so, the drug is helpful in one particular way. "It can cut down on impulse drinking," Dr. Desrosiers explained. "Two steps are involved instead of the fast one step." By that he meant a person taking Antabuse must first make the decision to quit taking it; that gives him time to consider the second step, drinking.

Several men in our dorm plan to take Antabuse. Mr. Wellington, of course, wants to. Johnny Ross, the moody man I've been jogging with, leaves the ARC tomorrow, and he's been taking the tablet four or five days. That's the general practice here; if a patient is to use Antabuse on the outside, he starts taking it here. The "Pilot" says he absolutely will take it. He's a dedicated man who has been through some hard years, including a previous trip here, but he seems to have fixed on the idea that he can still save himself—physically and mentally—if he gets off whiskey now. He doesn't fly any more, but he's been promised a job with an airline.

I've thought a lot about Antabuse and decided that I won't take it. I can't explain my feelings precisely, but they're something like this: I want not to drink for positive reasons—I'm already enjoying some of them—rather than being frightened off drinking. I also find it somehow insulting to my mind—that a pill in my belly can tell me what to do. Finally, it's as if I will have done a little better job patching myself up emotionally if I do it by myself.

Wednesday

✕

Wᴇʟᴅᴏɴ Bᴀʏʟɪss ᴍᴀᴅᴇ ɪᴛ ᴏғғɪᴄɪᴀʟ ᴛᴏᴅᴀʏ ᴛʜᴀᴛ four of us can leave tomorrow—Paul Evans, Luther Moore, Mr. Wellington, and I.

All of us are pleased, especially Mr. Wellington; he probably was surprised, too. But Bayliss had cleared us all, offering counsel at the group session this morning, then seeing us again this afternoon for individual conferences.

Looking at the file cards he has on each of us, Bayliss began the session. "Let's see . . . several of you are leaving tomorrow. And, Mr. Ross, you're leaving today."

"Yes, sir," Johnny Ross said. "Soon as I get out of this meeting. My mother and them are picking me up."

"How's it going to be?" Bayliss asked. "Do you see any problems?"

"No, sir. I'm not going to drink any alkyhol."

Always Johnny Ross says the sentence that way—"I'm not going to drink any alkyhol"—and, always, I find myself not believing him, perhaps because he never adds "why" or "how."

"Well, all of us wish you the best, Mr. Ross," Bayliss said. "We wish you success."

I spoke to Johnny Ross after the session, telling him goodbye and to take good care. He certainly looked better than the first morning I saw him, the day I took him to the cafeteria and he was shaking so bad that he could hardly eat the half-slice of bread and drink the iced tea.

After Johnny Ross, Bayliss turned to us and asked, one by one, how our long weekends had been. This was our first meeting since the holiday because Bayliss had been working yesterday with the husband-wife seminar.

"Mr. Evans?" he said.

"My wife and I are going back together," Paul said. "We're going to see a marriage counselor."

"Fine," Bayliss said. "Were you able to talk?"

"Yes, sir. The best in a long time."

"Mr. McIlwain?"

I told him of the cop incident and, briefly, of the camping trip.

"You handled it well," Bayliss said. "The *adult* was in charge."

Sitting next to me was Mr. Wellington. I hadn't told anyone of the beer and I wanted to see if Mr. Wellington would confess.

"Mr. Wellington?" Bayliss said. "How was your weekend?"

"Well, it was all right." He hesitated. "I didn't find my wife quite as well as . . . I had hoped." He paused again. "I drank some beer."

No one said anything for a moment, and Bayliss asked, "Why did you do that?"

"My niece brought her children over and they messed up the house. With my wife not well, I didn't want . . . to worry her and I straightened everything up. My niece does that all the time."

"Did you speak to her about it?" Bayliss asked.

"No . . . I didn't. She has a terrible temper and she doesn't like anyone to tell her what to do. But I spoke to my wife."

"Why?" Bayliss asked. "Did you want your wife to speak to your niece?"

"Well, my wife *likes* to have the children there."

"I used to live in the same town with my mother and stepfather," Coley Thompson said, "and they took me for granted. When I moved away, everything was fine. I'd come back for a visit and they'd say, '*Come in*, Coley.' I would move out of town, Mr. Wellington."

"Just move out?" Bayliss asked.

"I'd straighten the thing out or move," Coley said. "One way or the other."

"The doctor says my wife needs the company," Mr. Wellington said. "He says it's good to have the children visit."

"Mr. Wellington, you feel trapped," Julie Ryan

said. "The doctors say your wife needs the company of the children. You're a gentleman. You've been taught to have respect for your wife and you don't know what to do. I would feel as if I were being taken advantage of."

"Do you feel you're being used?" Bayliss asked.

"To a certain extent, yes."

"I see you as a passive man, Mr. Wellington," Bayliss said. "Do you feel inadequate to handle things? Here's a social situation that screams for action. Do you feel you can't handle it?"

"Yes, I guess so."

"Does *anybody* listen to you, Mr. Wellington?" Bayliss asked. The hour was gone and no one, Bayliss or a member of the group, had spoken again of Mr. Wellington's drinking the beer. As Bayliss summed up, directing his comments at Mr. Wellington, I felt that he was speaking to me, too:

"You've been pushed around, haven't you, Mr. Wellington? You've tried appeasement and that doesn't work. You wind up with resentment and depression, and you get drunk. You've got to experiment with new methods. So you bungle things—it's not the end of the world. Try something new."

Walking back to our dorm, Mr. Wellington said, "I guess I've got to be tougher."

"You've got to swing on 'em, Mr. Wellington," I said.

It struck me that we were ending the group sessions

almost as we had begun them—the day Tip Watson
said, "Hell, Mr. Wellington, if you got in a good first
lick you might whup some of those fellows."

Weldon Bayliss fills out a report on each of us
before we leave. It goes to Dr. Desrosiers, offering an
opinion on how Bayliss thinks we will fare. When I
went this afternoon to his office, he said, "I've enjoyed
having you in the group."

"I've enjoyed it, too," I said.

"How do you think you'll get along?" he asked.

"I guess I'll have a tough time," I said. "I'll worry
about my family."

"Yes," he said.

"But I'm not going to drink," I said. "Even if I
have a tough time."

"What are you going to do?"

"I don't know exactly. The publisher in Virginia
will give me fifteen hundred dollars to talk to his
people. After that I'll write until I get a job on a
newspaper. I can't make enough money writing to
put my children through college."

"Can you get a good job?"

"I don't know," I said. "People know I drank a
lot—they may be afraid."

"I hope you have good luck," he said. He looked
at some papers on his desk. "I'll tell you what I'm
going to say about you in my report. You're highly
motivated, highly intelligent. I would say your chances
of not drinking are quite good. But you've got a tough

row to hoe: no job, family problems, possible depression if your writing doesn't go well."

I told him that sounded pretty accurate to me and I thanked him for the days I had spent in his group. I have grown to like him. As I was about to leave, he said, "There's something you hear around AA—that you have to put sobriety ahead of everything. *Everything*. Family, job, everything. If that sounds selfish, what it means is that AA men have learned that if they lose sobriety they, in time, will lose everything."

Thursday

><

It was hot as we loaded the car in front of the administration building, carrying back all that I had brought—my books, the typewriter, two bags of clothing, a hundred newspapers, and two tennis rackets. Luther Moore and Mr. Wellington, who were going to ride with me, had lighter loads, and they helped me with mine. With his benign pink face and horseshoe of silver hair, Mr. Wellington looked happy as he strode down the white walk, smiling, carrying my steel Tensor racket in his left hand, the wooden Davis in his right. He swung the Davis a few times.

We said goodbye to several people as we made two trips from the dorm to the car. Mr. Leland and the Pilot were sitting on a bench out front, talking, and Julie Ryan was in the lobby. I put my hand on Mr. Leland's shoulder. "Let's go across the river, Mr.

Leland, and *get* one." He smiled. He still shakes, and
I suppose he always will. Julie looked good, fresh and
pressed in a blue and white print dress, some of the
taut lines of unhappiness gone, I thought, from her
face. She will be going home in a few days; we promised to stay in touch.

As we got into the car, Mr. Wellington said, "It's
been all right here. It's a good place."

I felt that way, too. I was glad to be going, but I
had spent happy, worthwhile days here. I liked the
people and the place.

"I was afraid they were going to hold me over," Mr.
Wellington said. "I appreciated Mr. Bayliss letting
me leave."

"I was glad you told him about the beer," I said.
"I was waiting to see if you would."

"I'm glad, too," Mr. Wellington said.

On Interstate 85, approaching the turnoff to where
Tip Watson works, I wished that we had time to stop
and see him, but we were running late. "I hope Tip's
getting along all right," I said.

"I do, too," Mr. Wellington said.

I had come to like Tip a great deal and understand
him, too, I think. I am going to try to see him when
I can. That afternoon when we sat on the grass with
our shirts off, talking, I was moved by the sadness of
Tip's life—and by the chance that he saw of my own
life being better. It took a deep hold on me, the
thought of a stranger who had failed wanting so much
to see me make it.

Luther Moore had been riding silently, cramped

beside his trunk, in the back seat. "Are you going back to the factory, Luther?" I asked.

"I don't want to," he said. "The noise gets me. But I may have to, until I can find something else."

"I hope I can get my old job back," Mr. Wellington said. "The social worker said she would help me try to get it."

As I had told Bayliss, I didn't know exactly what I was going to do. After the newspaper meetings in Virginia, I will find a place to live, maybe on a beach or in the mountains. In Virginia, I will get my first taste of what it's like to be in a room with everyone drinking whiskey except me. I have been to many newspaper gatherings and none was dry.

It will be the first time in four or five years that I have spoken while totally sober. Not long before I left New York, I interviewed a black nationalist on television after drinking six martinis. I'm not proud of it; it's just a fact. Now I'll have to see how well I can do business without gin.

Swinging west onto I-40, we were riding fast now, in silence, the windows rolled tight, the air conditioning on. Soon I would be dropping off Mr. Wellington, then Luther. I wondered how each of us would fare. I recalled the statistics: of three men who leave Butner, two fail and must return. One succeeds. To myself, I wished us all luck, but if numbers dog us, I want to be the one of three.

Toronto, Canada

—————⋈⋈⋈⋈⋈—————

Sunday

✠

I N PLACE AND TIME, I AM FAR FROM NORTH CAROLINA
and the hot afternoon that I drove west on Interstate
40, taking Luther Moore and Mr. Wellington home.
It is winter in a city that I had never seen, and I am
at work beside a window, watching snow fall on wet
streets. Two hundred and twelve days have passed,
many of them splendid, a few of them frightening. I
have not wanted to drink and I am pleased with my
life.

I have lived on Atlantic Beach, North Carolina,
and in Toronto. On the beach, although writing steadily, I fished, swam, dug clams, crabbed, played tennis,
and lay in the sun—answering to no one. That might
be considered an inconclusive test of living in the
real world. But I live now in a seventeenth-floor apartment in downtown Toronto, rising at six A.M., writing

for two hours before working a full day on the *Toronto Star*, puzzling over a nine-column newspaper that is foreign to me, having a managing editor ask (not unkindly), "Are you sure you want to go back into the big time? How do you know it won't get you all over again?"—making sure that I tell a reporter (as Weldon Bayliss would urge) that he has buried the lead of his story in his fifteenth paragraph, working with my right hip hurting some days as if it had been struck by an ax. And when I leave the newspaper long after dark, stepping directly into wind off Lake Ontario . . . well, then I feel that my world is as real as anyone else's.

As I rode on Interstate 40 that day, I had nothing certain in front of me except the two newspaper meetings. After them, I wasn't sure what I would do.

The meetings went well. I arrived at the first one during the cocktail hour, necessitating an explanation, it seemed to me, why I did not have on a necktie or suit and wanted only a Sprite. I had just got out of Butner, I said, a center for alcoholics. No one seemed to care much, one way or the other, except the owner of the chain of newspapers. He stayed to drink with me, having five ginger ales and explaining that it had been almost a year since he got out of a private clinic in Tennessee. "You'll find you drink a hell of a lot of ginger ale," he said.

That night in the hospitality room, a publisher from New Mexico said, "I've been watching you all day—

you don't seem *afraid*. Can I talk to you?" He had been drinking a good bit. "When you wanted some coffee, even when he [the owner] was talking, you got up and got it. It's like you've found something and you aren't afraid."

"I guess everybody's afraid," I said. "I'm just not as afraid as I used to be."

"But it's like you've *found* something," he said.

I hadn't gone on the road as an advance man for Butner, and it's not my style anyway, so I didn't give him a thumping message on uplift and sobriety. But I did tell him that New Mexico might have a place similar to Butner and that if he was bothered by his drinking he might consider going there. "I feel a lot better," I said. "Maybe you would, too." There have been similar incidents since that night, and I have said about the same thing. I don't want to be a preacher, springing out at friends and strangers with a message, but there is a euphoria—common among reformed drunks—that would lead me to testify that life is wonderful, I have been given a second chance.

Soon after the Virginia trip, Lee and I moved into an apartment on Atlantic Beach and attended a party given by young Marine Corps fliers. The room was dark except for flashing lights and psychedelic posters; hard rock filled the room like thick layers of wool rug. The men, if not all handsome, were well-built, the women young and pretty. Cold Duck was pressed into my hand and a pilot, drunk, not truculent but puzzled, shouted above the stereo that he didn't quite understand this business of being an alcoholic.

Was I trying to cut back, lay off awhile, or what? Wine's okay, isn't it? And why had I settled into a Godforsaken place like this? There's no future for the whole Southeast, he said. Dead. Backward. California's the place.

The entire evening I felt at ease—too much, actually, because I realized the feeling bordered on one of superiority: the strong man among fools. I don't want that.

A week later we went to a "gourmet dinner," as it was described—gin and tonics, cucumber salad, sauerbraten, red wine, followed by cigars and cognac. Spending evenings that way, without drinking, there could be a danger, I suppose, of becoming overconfident. But I keep in mind—always—the AA speaker at Butner who cautioned against ever thinking: Well, maybe I wasn't a *real* alcoholic, maybe I can drink again.

About two months after leaving Butner, I called Tip Watson and asked if he would come to the beach and spend a weekend with me. Tip said he would like that very much—that he was getting along fine and was anxious to see me. We agreed to meet at eleven o'clock Saturday night at the Sportsmen's Fishing Pier; Tip would have worked all that day before driving the two hundred miles to the beach. Lee asked what Tip might like to eat, and I told her that many days in the cafeteria line he would ask, "What's this today—possum?" A little before eleven Lee and I were at the pier, drinking coffee and watching fishermen from all over North Carolina. We waited until one A.M., but Tip didn't come. On Monday night I called his home, and his mother answered.

"He's out in the yard," she said.

"Could you get him for me? I'll hold."

"He's out in the yard."

"Will you just go to the door and call him?" I asked. "I'd really like to talk to him."

"He's sleep," she said.

"Well, will you just go call him?"

"If I got him," she said—and then she was silent. "He couldn't talk to you. He's been drinking since Saturday night."

After that I tried a couple times to reach him by phone and wrote to him twice. Then one night he called me, his voice so weak that I didn't recognize it. "You all right?" he asked. "You really all right?" He had just got out of the hospital. "I do want to see you," he said. "I'm sorry I let you down." We agreed to meet at eleven o'clock on the fishing pier.

But Tip didn't come that night, either. I have never heard from him again.

Wondering about other patients I had been with at Butner, I made telephone calls.

Julie Ryan was fine. She had a good vacation, camping, and goes regularly to AA meetings.

Ellen Hill was attending AA meetings with Julie.

Jack Durham, the writer, was back at ARC.

Rooster had one "little slip-up" but was going to AA.

The Pilot had worked a week and been drunk on wine.

Mr. Wellington hadn't been able to get his job back and had got sick drinking beer on top of Antabuse.

Counting Tip Watson, that was seven. In the seventy-three days since we had left Butner, five of seven had failed, to one degree or another.

Tip hurt the most because I liked him the best.

Eleven days before my forty-sixth birthday, I awoke on a Saturday morning in my Toronto apartment and found that I could not walk well. My steps were unsure and I bumped against a door. When I tried to brush my teeth, I could not direct the brush with my left hand, and changed to my right. In the mirror, I could see that the left side of my mouth had fallen, giving my face a strange, lopsided look. A cigarette slipped from my fingers, and I almost dropped a cup of coffee. My speech was slurred. I have always had fine health, even in the years when I drank, and I knew that I should go to a hospital; whatever had happened to me was not simple.

Lying on an emergency-room stretcher in Wellesley Hospital, trying to touch my nose and then a doctor's finger—with my left hand, I could not—I had many feelings. One was irony. *This is what happens? I quit drinking, make a good start—and it all falls apart so soon?* But fear was what I felt most: *how will I take care of my family? if I don't die, and surely I won't, no life insurance will be paid; but if I live and can't work, how will I take care of them? suppose the* Star,

*which gave me a chance, thinks, No, he's too risky—
an alcoholic and bad health, too? what will Lee feel
now? a beautiful young girl with an old man who is
sick; it is a long way from her life as a college girl; especially if I'm paralyzed.* "You've had a slight stroke,"
the doctor said. "You'll be all right. I'll call a neurol-
ogist. All of the effects should be gone tomorrow."

And all of them were—except the fear. It remained,
diminishing only gradually as good people helped me.
Lee and my mother and brother-in-law came twice
a day to visit during the week that I was in the hospital. The president of the *Star* wrote to me, saying,
"Take good care of yourself—we need you." And the
managing editor came to visit, bringing books. Lee
reacted just as she had when I went to Butner: I
would be all right, and so would she. Doctors, kind
men who talked with me each day—"Sure, you can
play tennis as soon as you get out"—made tests all
week and found nothing that had caused the stroke.
But the chances of a repetition were slight, they said,
and I should not worry.

I left the hospital on a Saturday and returned to
the *Star* on Monday. I can't say I did not worry about
the stroke—I did. I *do.* But I never feel the slightest
inclination—not ever—to try to ease the worry by
drinking, as I had for so many years with lesser worries.

Mostly, I try to put it out of my mind, enjoying
my job, the city, and Lee. She intends to go to
medical school and I have started work on a novel.
Both will be difficult, but I have come to believe in
many things. They are possible.

About the Author

WILLIAM McILWAIN was born in Lancaster, South Carolina, and has been a writer and newspaper editor all of his adult life. He was editor of *Newsday* until 1970, when he left to become writer-in-residence at Wake Forest University. Mr. McIlwain was a collaborator in the writing of *Naked Came the Stranger* and *Legends of Baptist Hollow*. He is the author of *The Glass Rooster*, a novel, and his writing appears frequently in leading American magazines. After he left Butner, Mr. McIlwain lived on a beach, fishing and writing this book. He is now the deputy managing editor of the *Toronto Star*.